Taking the Biscuit

Also by Faith Addis

The Year of the Cornflake
Green Behind the Ears
Buttered Side Down
Down to Earth

Taking the Biscuit

Faith Addis

ANDRE DEUTSCH

First published in Great Britain 1989
by André Deutsch Limited
105-106 Great Russell Street London WC1

British Library Cataloguing in Publication Data

Addis, Faith
Taking the biscuit.
I. Title
828'.91407

ISBN 0 233 98499 2

ISBN 0 233 98515 8 (Paperback edition)

Printed in Great Britain by
Ebenezer Baylis and Son Limited, Worcester

Chapter One

IN ISOLATED rural areas there are many elderly people who have difficulty getting their toenails cut. It's a fact. Bus services have been reduced so drastically that even if the old folk were mobile, which many are not, they find themselves living too far from a bus route to be able to make the journey into town. And another fact, surprising in view of the unemployment figures, is that there is a shortage of chiropodists.

I learned all this while I was bathing old Mrs Sinclair's dog Jingle. It seemed ironic that isolated rural *dogs* could get home visits from travelling groomers like me, but not their owners. Mrs Sinclair was not quite infirm enough to qualify for a district nurse and had to manage as best she could with the help of her neighbour Flo, who came in once a week. 'She stops me drowning while I have my bath,' Mrs Sinclair explained. 'She sits on a chair on the landing and we talk through the door. If I stopped talking she'd come in and see to me.' Since Flo herself was as old and frail as Mrs Sinclair it was hard to see how she could be of any practical help apart from pulling out the bath plug.

'And who helps Flo with her bath?' I asked.

'I do of course. Every Tuesday I go to Flo's and every Friday she comes to me. Her son bought her some mixer taps with a shower attachment,' she added, not enviously but with a sort of reflected glory. Privately I thought the son needed a kick up the backside. Mixer taps were all very well but Flo's cottage walls were peeling, the garden was overgrown and, worst of all, Flo had no telephone.

'So we keep ourselves decent,' Mrs Sinclair went on, 'and if it wasn't for our blessed toenails we'd be all right.'

By this time I had finished towelling Jingle dry. I had

trimmed his coat before he had his bath and all that now remained was to clip his claws. I should have been alert to all the hints Mrs Sinclair had been throwing out but I wasn't and her next remark caught me unprepared. 'When you've finished Jingle's would you do mine?'

The full horror of the request didn't strike me immediately. I concentrated hard on Jingle's paws, taking longer than was necessary in order to gain time to think. Unsterilised instruments . . .? Hippocratic oath . . .? No, that wouldn't wash, she'd know it doesn't apply to dogs . . . oh *help*.

When I turned round Mrs Sinclair had removed her stockings. The nails in question had grown over into massive horny talons, thick and corrugated and evidently very painful. I could hardly tell her that she needed a farrier. Inspiration struck. 'It's an offence', I said priggishly, 'to pretend to be medically qualified when you're not.'

'You make it sound like an abortion.' Mrs Sinclair shook with laughter at her own wit. 'It's only a few toenails. Please?'

'No,' I said, feeling very mean at not even having a try. But if word got round that the 'dog lady' did feet, heaven help me. It wouldn't stop at Mrs S and Flo. All their cronies would come hobbling along followed by a queue of solicitors waving writs for blood poisoning. 'It's dangerous,' I said. 'I'm sorry, but without the right instruments I could do more harm than good. Now, I've finished Jingle so I must be going.' I picked up my bag and opened the door.

'Poor Jingle,' said Mrs Sinclair.

I shut the door and came back in. 'What do you mean poor Jingle? What's wrong with him?'

'He's too fat.'

I said Jingle would be all right if he didn't have so many snacks between meals. Mrs Sinclair said it wasn't the snacks it was lack of exercise. How could she take him for walks with her blessed feet?

My idea of a perfect world would be one where the only

2

humans were toddlers or old people. Everyone else could go into deep freeze in between these stages, leaving the actual running of the planet to dolphins or honorary dolphins like David Attenborough. As this is unlikely to happen in the foreseeable future, people have to get on with things as they are, with everybody aiming for their own particular goal at their own particular speed. This would be fine if all the players were facing the same way but they're not. A traffic warden trying to notch up twenty parking tickets a day is certainly not playing the same game as his twenty motorists who in their turn could be burglars with nothing in common with their twenty victims, and so on almost indefinitely.

In a bid to play the game at a more leisurely pace Brian and I moved from London to the West Country in the mid-seventies and had experimented with several ways of earning a living since then. Brian had taught himself a tremendous amount about horticulture, I had become a trained 'dog lady' and we both knew quite a lot about animal husbandry. During this quest for knowledge we had moved house five times and have the tidiest cupboards of anyone I know – junk simply doesn't have time to accumulate – and a cat whose fur comes up like a bottle brush if she sees a tea chest.

After two years in the wilderness (Dartmoor) where our beautiful but semi-derelict cottage kept us endlessly busy, we moved down again to the lowlands. Dartmoor had been marvellous, but for the serious horticulturist it was a bit cold, with hard frosts right into May, then a short summer then cold again by late August. Healthy for humans but murder for plants.

The new place by contrast was tailor-made for plants. Five inter-connecting south-facing glasshouses. (Our own quarters were adequate but not noteworthy.) These were not greenhouses in the 'Garden Centre' sense where everything is pot grown and the glass merely a form of shelter, but Victorian kitchen garden glasshouses, once an essential annexe to every grand house. Huge cast-iron pipes led from a boilerhouse and ran along brick walls all round the growing areas. It must have been lovely in the olden days going in there on a cold winter's morning and having a warm up on the pipes before starting work. The main growing areas were raised soil beds. When we first went to view the property we were so taken with the raised beds we made an offer on the spot. Brian, rather awed, said 'This could mean the end of backache as we know it,' little guessing how accurately this would describe 'raised-bed backache'. You get the same amount of pain but higher up – fibrositis instead of lumbago. Still, it made a change. Some of the beds were edged with thick terracotta tiles, each about a foot square and faded with age to a beautiful pale apricot. There was also a chest containing hundreds of tiny clay pots, hand-thrown according to a potter friend and which still had the imprints of someone's thumb. After this discovery I kept bringing glasshouse oddments indoors to wash, convinced that every article was historic until Brian unkindly squashed my optimism. 'It says Made in Taiwan,' he'd say, or 'Woolworths, circa 1950,' and out would go another potential treasure.

It was mid-summer when we moved in, too late to start any growing programmes. So the whole glasshouse block stood empty while we did other things like clearing up the land for the two ponies and decorating the house. A friend of ours called Terry, who with his wife Joy and sister-in-law Pat, had put in a noble day's work on moving day, pointed out that the house needed rewiring. Terry had trained as an electrician during his National Service and knew a frayed end when he saw one. We were downcast at the prospect of the unplanned expense then upcast again when Terry said he would show Brian how to do it himself. He lent Brian a stack of books on electricity and also gave him a list of all the materials needed for the job.

The books were so boring I marvelled at how anybody could bear to write them let alone read them. But Brian ploughed through the lot, making notes as he went along and obviously looking forward to mastering a new skill. To date our only brush with electricity had been trying to outwit electrically-fenced pigs and ponies who all seem to be born with a physics degree. But as I was going to be electrician's mate I made a show of interest in the books, all put on. I did learn that volts are so called after a Greek called Volta discovered them and that Edison's middle name was Alva (what a weird name) but all the stuff about positive and negative particles was so yawn-making I gave up.

Brian assembled all the necessary rolls of cable, switches and so forth then phoned Terry to say he was ready to start. Terry and Joy came round – they only lived a few minutes' drive away – and while Terry and Brian prepared to do muffled things in the loft, Joy and I were given our orders. Electricians' mates are not as subordinate as I had thought. (And hoped.) They are expected to make the tea of course but they also have to act as tracker dogs. A man crawling about on the loft rafters doesn't actually know where he is in relation to the rooms below unless someone stands underneath and shouts bathroom or front bedroom, etc. Joy and I were issued with bamboo canes to tap on the ceilings, first to guide the elevated pair to the place in each ceiling where the light fitting lives and then to poke up into the holes which they drilled when they got there. To rewire a lighting circuit you lay the new cables alongside the old ones and make exit holes a few inches away from the old ceiling roses. 'Why,' I asked Joy as we picked bits of powdered ceiling out of our hair, 'do we have to leave the canes in the holes?' The place was beginning to look like an upside-down runner-bean support.

'It's called looping in,' said Joy who had plainly done this before. 'Terry and Brian wouldn't know where they'd drilled if they didn't have a marker for each hole. They'll run the new wire to each cane soon and make loops for us to pull down into the rooms.'

Oh well, ask a silly question. I still had the notion that light was provided by some sort of divine intervention between the switch and the bulb. The activities of our heroes in the loft soon put paid to that idea. 'Looping in' sounded more like a twelve-round boxing match between two heavyweights. There were thuds and grunts and oaths. I thought perhaps Brian had not got beyond Volta the Greek in the textbook either. Of course they were working in the dark which didn't help and Terry was further handicapped by being exceptionally tall. To jolly things along Terry called down 'Grab hold of this wire, would you,' which I did; then he called again, 'You all right?' When I said I was he said 'That's a relief. Whatever you do don't touch the other one.' I nearly had heart failure before I realised it was a joke.

Some time later they crawled down, hot and sweaty and covered in loft dust. They had made a start, they informed us. 'You mean there's *more*?' I said, aghast that all the noise and falling plaster was only a start. But there was a lot more, about ten days of the same. Terry would start Brian off on the next stage of the job and leave him to finish it, then start another stage. Brian found ceiling connections the hardest part of the job partly because he was working above his head but mainly because each fitting had about a million tiny wires which *all* had to be screwed in correctly. There were ten ceiling lights and twenty plug sockets not counting the cooker point.

At last the day came when it was time to switch on. I am ashamed to say that I never believed any of it would actually work, in fact I was so sure the whole place would become an instant cinder directly the switch was thrown that I put on rubber gloves and wellingtons for the ceremony. Terry said caustically that he'd like to meet the idiot who gave me such an inappropriate name. Brian switched on. Ten ceiling lights obediently lit up and various appliances connected to the new circuit for the test came on. The wheel in the meter whizzed round as fast as an extractor fan and we were absolutely cock-a-hoop. In our experience hardly anything goes according to plan and definitely not a major project in a hitherto unknown field. While we were waiting for the Electricity Board man (they always have to check new installations for safety) we put the electric kettle on and made a celebratory cup of tea. When the man came he wasn't in the least interested to hear about my brilliant husband and friend but only whether the work was up to the Board's standard.

It was of course and the success quite went to Brian's head. He built himself a propagator in one of the greenhouses and wired it up to the mains. That worked as well, crumbs – *two* victories in a

6

row. A heated propagator in a greenhouse which was already hot enough to grow dates in seemed to be a fairly pointless exercise but Brian said it would save him having to do it in the autumn. He filled the tray to a depth of two inches with silver sand and enclosed the whole thing with a polythene tent. We had a new cat, Mitzi, who had come with the house (her owners had moved near a main road and didn't want to risk her being run over) and when Mitzi discovered the propagator she went into ecstasies. 'A summerhouse of my own,' she purred, and rolled over and over in the silver sand. She was a tabby and must have felt nicely camouflaged in the grey stuff. Having rearranged the surface to her satisfaction and to Brian's apprehension, she curled up in a ball and went to sleep. Brian told her she could have a short lease on the place but would have to vacate it when it was time to plant seeds. 'But if I find you using it as a loo, you're out,' he warned. Mitzi, being a most co-operative cat, listened carefully and for the next couple of months continued to treat her summerhouse with great respect.

Our own cat, Small, did not like having another cat in the family and from the start would growl threateningly at Mitzi. It was a situation not unlike that of having a new baby and a jealous elder child. If they had been children we would have turned to Spock for guidance but as there wasn't anything remotely like a Spock-for-Cats book in the library we sided with Mitzi. Some psychologists say that the way humans treat cats is an indication of their unconscious feelings about themselves. I don't know what such experts would have made of the way we solved the Small/Mitzi conflict. It seemed so unfair to let Small go on hissing and spitting at someone so good-natured; we would chuck our slippers at Small and send her outside until her temper had cooled. This probably means that our unconsciouses are in a dreadful mess but from a practical point of view it did the trick.

The dogs took the move in their stride as always. As long as they have their bean-bags and us they don't seem to mind upheavals. The ponies were happy too, with clean pasture and a fresh view. And although we don't normally bother to move any plants other than potted ones, on this occasion I brought with us sixteen cowslips which I had raised from seed and wanted to hang on to. If I had known then what loose morals these innocent looking plants possess I think I would have left them behind. But in my ignorance I planted them in a shady spot ready to give us a nice display the following spring and forgot about them.

As it was the wrong time of year for Brian to start anything interesting in the glasshouses he decided to get a job. For a person who has been self-employed all his adult life this could have been quite traumatic, but Brian was lucky. The work – for want of a better word – he chose was exploring rural Devon on foot. The job description didn't actually say 'walking round Devon' but that's exactly what it was. A national project had been set up to locate all the old green lanes (a green lane is an unmetalled road bordered by ancient banks and hedges) still in use, and to feed the information to a central computer so that up-to-date maps could be drawn. Several teams of 'surveyors' were required to carry out the work and each team had to include an experienced driver who was used to driving minibuses. Brian applied and was taken on as a surveyor/driver.

Once they had found the lanes the teams had to observe and record everything they could about them: the bank formations, numbers and species of animals, ditto plants. Each person was equipped with a grown-up version of the I Spy Things in the Country books to enable them to identify rare plants and to tell the difference between fox and badger droppings. Some of the things spied upon were never recorded. When the new updated maps are published the footnotes will tell of barn owl habitats, of butterflies, moles and weasels, and of all the wonderful summer flowering plants, but nowhere will you find otters recorded, or bank managers enjoying a lunchtime frolic with their secretaries. The Green Laners were conservationists to the core.

Based in the grounds of Dartington near Totnes, the office of the green lanes project was a wooden hut. It was a very nice hut situated in a woodland clearing, a suitable Alma Mater for Brian. Each day the teams would be allotted locations to be mapped and off they would go, in a convoy of terrible old minibuses. How any of these vehicles got through the MOT was a mystery. Doors flew open, oil belched out of the exhausts, brakes failed, and on one occasion a steering wheel came off in the driver's hands. I was always very relieved to see Brian arrive safely home each evening. We are no strangers to old bangers, the most we have ever paid for a car is £600, but the green lanes vans had to be seen to be believed. Brian used to get to work early so as to have the best choice, a rather fine distinction, like choosing between two dinosaurs. There was a blue one which always gave the driver backache because there was no stuffing left in the upholstery, a white one which stuck in gear and some others with engines so tired they would die at the first hill and have to be towed back to the hut.

The workforce was drawn mainly from the Totnes area. One or two were people between jobs like Brian, and a few were school leavers waiting to go up to university. But the majority were what we soon came to recognise as true Totnes-ites, not dropouts or they wouldn't have been working no matter how attractive the job, but practising non-conformists as refreshingly different as the Hampstead bohemians of the 1960's. They dressed in a style something between moulting yak and Oxfam, the hairy garments being adorned with Red Indian thongs and beads. They were all heavily into self-enlightenment as I learned when Brian brought some of them home for coffee once. Naturally I knew better than to offer them coffee or tea. Our son Marcus, a member of the alternative society himself had, after his last visit home, left behind a selection of alternative beverages; limeflower and hibiscus mix, Celestial Season (brand name) drink, carob cup, all sounding irresistible and all tasting like silage. Although I didn't serve them in home-thrown pottery mugs (one has to draw the line somewhere) and could only offer bone china, the nauseous brews were eagerly accepted and Brian got a lot of kudos for having an enlightened wife.

Totnes, we were told, was where it was at. In the rarefied south Devon air, particularly if you lived near a ley line, you could rediscover your essential self and once you had done that

9

you could radiate goodwill in ever-increasing ripples.

'How?' I said, topping up one of the yaks with Celestial Season.

'By example,' he – or it may have been she – said. 'By sharing rather than competing, by spiritually connecting, by recognising that the female force inside every being has the power to radiate—'

'Yes,' I interrupted, not wishing to hear about the radiating ripples twice. 'I meant how do you rediscover your essential self?'

Brian sighed and looked at his watch. It was one of those quaint old-fashioned ones that tell the time, very untrendy compared to the totally blank ones worn by some of our guests. (Time is an illusion . . .)

'And why *re*discover?' I persisted. 'If you've discovered yourself once why do it again?'

The group radiated ripples of goodwill towards me and all talking at once explained about Gestalt therapy, Reich, bio-energetics, personal astrology and rebirthing. It sounded exhausting particularly the rebirthing which involves being immersed in a tub of water for half a day while you do deep-breathing exercises. Totnes, which Brian had already visited but I had not, came across as a centre of slightly unbalanced people in search of a guru or, in the case of rebirthers, a bath. I was reminded of a girl I used to know called Dora who moved to Totnes.

Dora was conceived in 1942 in a London air-raid shelter. Her mother, Rose, then aged eighteen was hurrying home one evening in the blackout when the sirens went off. Rose was very frightened and screamed in panic until an A.R.P. warden rescued her and conducted her to the safety of the nearest shelter. The shelter turned out to be empty so instead of leaving Rose to sit out the raid on her own, the helpful warden stayed with her and introduced her to a pastime guaranteed to take a girl's mind off the blitz. When the all-clear went the couple parted, never to meet again.

Not an unusual story in wartime but what was unusual

10

was what happened to Dora when she herself reached the age of eighteen. History repeated itself. This time the action took place not in an air-raid shelter but in a cave during a thunderstorm. Dora was on a cycling holiday in the Pyrenees when suddenly there was a loud bang of thunder followed by torrential rain. Dora took to some nearby caves and met up with another refugee from the storm, one Jean-Claude, a student by trade, very French, very dark and very handsome. Not however, very careful and a Catholic to boot.

Nine months later Bernadette was born, a beautiful memento of Dora's holiday. Grandmother Rose was overjoyed and made immediate arrangements for the three of them to leave the then smog-ridden London and move to the country.

She bought a cottage in Wales but although the air was cleaner the puritanical villagers made the family's life miserable so they moved again. This time their new home was a tumbledown cottage near Totnes and they loved it. Even as far back as the Sixties Totnes had a reputation for its 'good vibes' and an illegitimate child or two made no difference to the warmth of the welcome newcomers received. Rose and Dora both took part-time jobs and spent their spare time restoring the cottage. Bearded boyfriends moved in. Dora used to say 'There's nothing like our granite slabs for separating the men from the boys.'

Baby Bernadette thrived. On her first day at playgroup she came home and told the family she had learned a song called 'The Towel and the Pillowcase Went To Sea in a Beautiful Pea-green Boat'. Dora took her to the clinic to have her ears tested and also to a clairvoyant in Plymouth to have her horoscope read. Both authorities agreed that the child was highly intelligent, one finding that she had a flair for spatial and mathematical concepts and the other that she would have a long and successful life with twin boys somewhere in the picture.

After Bernadette's eighteenth birthday her mother and grandmother waited with interest to see whether the genetic tendency to become pregnant in a crisis would make itself apparent for the third time. Rose bet Dora five pounds that the twin boys

11

would put in an appearance before the year was up, and Dora, who was by now into Tarot card reading, accepted the bet. She foresaw foreign travel for Bernadette with some exciting underwater treasure trove at the end of it. Bernadette confounded her family by winning a scholarship to London University to read pure mathematics.

'What a lovely story,' said a lad called Fil. (Not short for Philip but Filbert, a self-chosen 'in' name for Totnes-ites.) 'Did Bernadette have the twins?'

'I don't know,' I said. 'I lost touch with Dora years ago.'

'Thank God,' Brian muttered. He had suffered mightily from some of my friends in London including one girl who had asked for a bed for the night and then stayed six months. The party broke up and arguing mildly among themselves over the use of Tarot cards, they all went home.

'Matey lot, aren't they?' said Brian.

'Mm, very. You're lucky to have such a nice bunch to work with. Was the one in the orange bathmat male or female?'

'Bee? She's got four children.'

'Four? She doesn't look old enough. Is the Bee as in sting or Beatrice?'

'As in honey. I think her real name is Susan.'

There's a lot to be said for moving house apart from the tidy cupboards I mentioned earlier. If you want to see how the other half lives there is no better way than moving near their territory. We had no idea there was a thriving community of New Age people in south Devon. (In case of misunderstanding, I *don't* include unwashed dropouts who roam the countryside in old lorries and cause nothing but trouble.) As an addict of the late Goon Show I loved the idea of everyone changing their names and looking for themselves as a way of life. And as a realist I wish we had thought of starting a business to service their needs. Our friends come and stay with us and get plunged in mud for nothing; what short-sighted fools we were not to call it Cosmic Mud and charge self-discoverers ten pounds an hour to sit in the stuff. Other entrepreneurs do it. We heard of one 'rebirthing' business that charges forty pounds an hour for the tub-of-water torture. They include a cup of something (I dread to think what) in the price.

Coincidentally, shortly after we became aware of the interest in off-beat practices, Brian saw an advert in the local paper for someone to set up and run a kitchen garden to serve a guest-house. He phoned for details and learned that the guest-house was one of those 'therapy' set-ups where the patients go for a weekend to find themselves. The proprietor wanted to offer them organically grown salads and vegetables. Would Brian care to come and inspect the proposed site? Brian would and so would his wife.

One of the first tests the patients were given was not so much an exercise in finding themselves as in finding the premises. There were no signposts. Eventually we arrived at the right place, a series of prefabricated huts amid builders' rubble. We knocked on one of the doors and a man of about thirty came out. He had dreadlocks and bare feet. Brian introduced himself and the man said, 'I shall have to ask you to remove your shoes.' This didn't sound too unreasonable in view of the mess outside so we did. But inside, instead of carpets, all we could see were bare boards and these were so gritty it didn't seem as though anybody else had taken their shoes off. The man led us through a kitchen area and then through what he called a dormitory only there were no beds, then into a sitting room. Steaming on a piece of string hung above a coal fire (this was July) were three pairs of socks. 'You can sit down if you like,' said the man. 'I'll get John to make you some tea.'

'No thanks,' we said, having seen the kitchen. We looked round for chairs but the place seemed strangely underfurnished and we ended up on bean-bags. I said I hoped his dogs wouldn't mind and the man said they didn't have a dog. Then a young man came in, barefoot and carrying a saucepan full of brown rice which he proceeded to eat with his fingers straight from the saucepan. Brian seemed mesmerised by the steaming socks so I said conversationally, 'When are you planning to open?'

13

'Open what?' said the man.

'The guest-house.'

'Oh, we've been open a couple of years.' Seeing how mystified we were at the lack of furniture he explained that he conducted 'encounter groups' at weekends. Apparently what you have to encounter in these sessions is each other, sometimes naked, sometimes blindfold, and furniture would only get in the way.

'But what do they sleep on?' I asked, picturing a mound of pink bodies huddled together for warmth. Futons were what they slept on, those incredibly uncomfortable hairy mats that nursery-school children were made to rest on in the bad old days. Things were going very well, the man told us (specially your bank balance, I thought) with the Centre fully booked for the current year. 'But I must have a reliable supply of organically grown produce for the guests,' he added. 'I've got the land and it seems wasteful not to use it. I'll show you.'

We padded across the grit again, found our shoes and walked the half mile or so to the proposed kitchen garden. The 'land' turned out to be a north-facing disused tennis court, shoulder high in nettles and surrounded on all four sides by netting. There was no aspect that escaped the wind and no water supply. When Brian pointed out these deficiencies his prospective employer seemed surprised that they *were* deficiencies. Brian, who was by now very annoyed at being brought out on a wild goose chase, said meaningly that whereas people might be able to go without basic comforts, plants certainly could not. And with that we left.

These places *are* therapeutic, there's no doubt about it. You feel better directly you leave and once you get home to carpets and chairs you feel positively euphoric. As for eating off plates, well, that's the icing on the cake. . . .

Chapter Two

DESPITE THE STERLING efforts of young upwardly mobile cranks I don't think they will ever be in the same league as the true old-fashioned British eccentric. Sadly, with the destruction of their habitat – the crumbling pile – these spirited old folk are an endangered species. Some are still with us, clinging to the wreckage of their ancestral homes, eking out pensions by selling eggs or illegal milk at the back door but there are precious few and we should cherish them. Particularly the ones without television sets. There is a TV programme called *The Antiques Road Show*, a good programme in most respects except that it will insist on putting a cash value on the items displayed. Many's the busybody who, after watching the programme, will suddenly recall that Lady Alice has a Meissen dish exactly like the one valued at X pounds which she uses for the ducks' food. Before they know what's happening Lady Alice's ducks find themselves beak-deep in a plastic washing-up bowl while their lovely old dish goes off to gather dust in a museum. There *are* Lady Alices who are women of principle (our ninety-year-old friend Victoria rears runt piglets in a Jacobean chest because, as she says, the Jacobeans knew about insulation) but they tend to be outnumbered by the busybodies.

This is not to say you can't be eccentric on a housing estate but it's far harder. There was a man living in an isolated farmhouse in Somerset who disliked the colour yellow. There were no yellow flowers in his garden and if he spotted a person on his land wearing yellow he would get out his old army pistol and fire a few warning shots in the air. Nobody in the neighbourhood minded his little habit (except maybe Telecom engineers new to the job) whereas if he had lived in a town his behaviour would have been regarded as odd and social workers might have felt obliged to do something.

Or take my mother. (Double Green Shield Stamps if you do.) When she lived in the country her conversations with her pets went unnoticed. Not so when she moved into town. 'Inky thinks it's Tuesday,' she would say to baffled shoppers. 'I've told her we've already had Tuesday this week but she will argue.' The shoppers would withdraw nervously while Anne continued to reason with Inky, a single-minded dog who lived in hope that every day was Tuesday because that was the day the butcher gave out free bones.

There are of course degrees of eccentricity. My job as a mobile dog-clipper brings me into contact with people ranging from dull conformists to the frankly mad and in a curious way these two extremes are not unconnected. For example in the first household – let's call them Mr and Mrs Boring – there is a definite under-current of madness which I personally find a bit scary. You ring the doorbell, wait while two or three bolts are undone, and are admitted into a fawn-coloured hall with a fawn carpet. There may or may not be a plastic houseplant at this point. Following Mr Boring (drip-dry shirt, polyester trousers and slippers) through to the kitchen you are struck by the absence of anything connected with *living*. No trays of seedlings thrusting through on the windowsill, no crockery – it's all been shut behind formica cupboard doors – no magazines or papers, no sounds of homemade plonk fermenting, nothing to focus on except a glimpse of the garden seen through a screamingly clean net curtain. The dog, the object of the visit, will almost invariably turn out to be not the Borings' own dog but someone else's that they're minding. They want it washed and clipped, not for its own comfort but to 'save trouble'. Although they don't say so they would actually prefer to have it killed and stuffed.

As I say, I find the Borings' madness scary. Their fear of untidiness, dirt, what-the-neighbours-might-think, communicates itself to me and I do my work as quickly as possible and go. If I've arranged my day right my next call will be antidotal, to a home with that comforting 'freshly burgled' look, where mermaids in the bath and unicorns grazing outside are the norm.

*

16

One of Brian's workmates was a twenty-three-year-old called Matthew Morgan. He had been a green laner for six months and was leaving shortly to start his own business. 'You'd like Matthew,' Brian said. 'He's going in for worm farming.'

'Lucky him,' I said. I had been interested in worms for years but had never had the chance to meet a professional. 'Can you get us invited over, Brian? Would Matthew mind?'

'Of course he wouldn't mind, I told him you'd probably want to see the wormery when it's set up and he said he'd give me a ring in a few weeks.'

While we were waiting for the invitation I looked out all my old worm books. There wasn't much; Darwin still holds pride of place (as far as I know) with his definitive Earthworm treatise and I also had some booklets issued by commercial wormeries. These gave practical guidance on husbandry but I suspected they glossed over any snags. One instruction leaflet stated: 'Happy worms will not leave home.' In other words a worm farmer can sleep easy, knowing his charges will stay within bounds as long as they are happy. But what makes a worm happy? I would have to ask Matthew. After some years of keeping the sort of livestock who spent their entire lives figuring out the best way to crash through stock-proof hedges the idea of home-loving creatures sounded too good to be true.

One day the invitation from Matthew came. Brian had said Matthew was a 'nice chap'. What he failed to mention was that the nice chap was a handsome six footer with green eyes and a lovely smile. (Perhaps he hadn't noticed.) Matthew was further endowed with a quick sense of humour and an intelligence which made him seem older than twenty-three. Every mother's dream son-in-law. What a pity Sara was so firmly based in London and was just starting a new relationship. . .

'. . . the red worm, or Eisinia Foetida,' Matthew was saying. I tore myself away from my fantasy in which Sara and Matthew plus their fifteen beautiful children were living in a luxurious manor house and running an international worm export business.

Matthew's present accommodation was a caravan. It was

17

rather crowded on the day of our visit. There was a telephone engineer repairing a faulty line, a man from Cornwall who had called to borrow worm-farming literature, us and Matthew. It was going to be a longish hop from this to the manor house notwithstanding Matthew's drive and energy. 'Come on,' he said, 'I'll show you the workers.'

Worm farming is a relatively new industry and is divided into two separate branches. Some wormeries go in for breeding only, and sell the live worms to various outlets – fishermen, gardeners and other worm farms. The second branch (Matthew's) is compost making. There is a limitless demand for natural composts. The Ministry of Agriculture, twenty years behind the times as usual, has recently woken up to the fact that chemical horticulture is not such a wonderful idea and has started to give encouragement and grants to would-be wormeries. With the help of a small grant Matthew had set up business in some stone barns, destined at a later date to be converted into a house for himself.

The compost beds were sited on concrete and enclosed on all four sides by wooden planks built up to a height of about three feet. Each bed contained approximately a ton of cow muck and straw plus its quota of worms at a stocking rate of 160 worms per square foot of surface area. The process of 'quick' (i.e. worm- worked) compost is to turn rotting vegetable matter into friable odourless humus in about six weeks. Obviously, decaying vegetation can be composted by other means but worm turning is quickest and the resulting compost is further enriched by the worms' own enzymes and bacteria. Passing through two sets of guts, first the cow then the worm, gives a fertiliser of such strength that it can't be used neat; it would be like us eating jars of Bovril at a sitting.

We saw just four beds on our first visit, from the raw starter bed to number four where the compost was finished and ready for sale. Brian and I ran our fingers through the lovely stuff and sniffed it appreciatively. Brian wanted to know how it was mixed and bagged and I wanted to know how Matthew got the worms out ready for their next assignment. 'Do you sieve the compost to get them out?' I asked.

'No,' said Matthew, 'That would take too long. I've trained them to come when I call the register.'

'They've all got different names then?'

'Yep. There's Willy and Wally and Wanda and Sydney (he's adopted) and Webster and Wyn – I get jolly tired after I've called all two hundred thousand of them I can tell you.'

We were giggling so much I forgot to ask him how he really did it and we moved on to the last stage of the processing. Being so concentrated the worm casts had to be carefully shredded and mixed with peat and sand to get the right balance before being bagged up. Matthew had been doing all the mixing by shovel but now that the compost was coming off the assembly line by the hundredweight he had invested in a shredder rather like a small cement mixer. It was still very hard work though, shovelling the ingredients in and then bagging up by hand. Matthew's surname being Morgan, he called his compost Morganic and had had white plastic bags designed with the name and a clever little worm logo. The whole set up was so neat and so ecologically essential – without worms the planet would be as dead as the moon – that I was hooked. I wanted a wormery.

As soon as we got into the car to go home after our conducted tour Brian forestalled my great idea. 'No,' he said, before I had even said a word.

'Why not?'

'Well, think about it. What's Matthew got that we haven't?'

'Youth and beauty.'

'Has he?' said Brian in surprise. (I *knew* he hadn't noticed.)

'He's got green eyes,' I said.

'Forget the eyes. He's got cow manure.'

'We've got horse manure.'

Brian sighed and said that even if we kept our two ponies in a permanent state of panic they couldn't possibly manufacture enough dung to feed a commercial wormery. I could see the sense in that. One of the drawbacks of moving house is that you have to leave your muckheap behind. I decided to wait until we had a good-sized heap again before reintroducing the subject of worms. It did seem a pity though to have had my interest aroused and then frustrated. Maybe I should start a secret wormery and surprise Brian by becoming big in the worm world, like a woman we had read about in the local paper who was selling 50,000 worms a week. Maybe not though, he'd be bound to find out.

Men are not easy to deceive. If you scorch his best sweater or give away what he thinks is his best sweater to a jumble sale, he will find out. Serious crimes, like using chisels as screwdrivers or letting cold air into his propagator have been known to lead to Really Bad Trouble, and very serious crimes to divorce. ('It is alleged, m'lud, that the plaintiff's wife did remove the television fuse in order to prevent the plaintiff from watching *Question Time*.')

Since most of us, however much we might dislike that noisy Robin Day, don't want to go to all the bother of training a fresh husband, we try our best to keep the peace by being careful. Careful that he doesn't find out I mean. We replace mangled chisels, sift earth over hoof-shaped craters in the herbaceous border and lie like hell when all else fails. What we don't do, ever, is go *looking* for trouble.

So when I heard, through friends, about a friend of theirs called Barbara who had an honours degree not only in looking for trouble but in getting away with it I couldn't wait to meet this superior being. According to our friends, Barbara had successfully hidden a flock of sheep from her husband. Surely not a *flock* of sheep, I thought, our friends must have got it wrong. Maybe an orphan lamb or two, only goodness knows that would be difficult enough what with the four-hourly feeds and the bleating.

But a flock it was. Our mutual friends introduced us and Barbara told me herself. It seemed the husband was not the Victorian ogre I had pictured but a quiet, average sort of chap who demanded nothing more than a quiet, average sort of life in town. It was the 'in town' that had made Barbara restless. She had been brought up in the country (her parents bred rhubarb) but as her husband needed to live near his office in town she had accepted the situation and settled down to urban life as best she could. They had two children, a boy and a girl who both grew up to be professional dancers and who, amazingly, *didn't* go through the usual adolescent phase of playing one parent off against the other. A sheep-secreting mother would be a sitting target for the sort of teenagers most of us have but luckily for Barbara hers were exceptionally nice. 'In fact,' she said, 'I couldn't have managed without them at times.' Their dancing training had made them strong and muscular, just the job for restraining heavy ewes at drenching time.

It was after the children had left school and embarked upon their training that Barbara had been bitten by the smallholding bug. Caught between two generations doing interesting things – the rhubarb parents and the dancing children – and having an office-orientated husband who came home for lunch, things must have looked dull. So for starters Barbara bought a pony and installed it on rented grazing out of town. The husband made a fuss: it would take up too much time, etc. – time which, by implication, could be better spent doing all the exciting things housewives love doing like washing, ironing, shopping, cooking and cleaning. Barbara calmed him down and fitted the pony into the domestic routine so that he hardly knew it existed.

A pony on its own gets lonely and soon it was joined by another pony and also a goat which needed a good home. This time the husband was not told about the new arrivals, there seemed no point, Barbara said, in inviting a row.

Things would have probably stayed like that if Barbara had not started going to evening classes in spinning and weaving. She had always been interested in sheep but suddenly the interest grew into a determination to have some real sheep of her own. She took the leap shortly afterwards and, never one to do things by halves, bought twenty pregnant ewes. Overnight life was far from dull. Firstly, Barbara knew very little about sheep management and had to learn from books. Secondly, the trips out of town to see the pony (still singular as far as the husband knew) now had to be extended to make sure everything was well with the sheep. And thirdly, letters from the Ministry of Agriculture had to be kept out of sight. Even the dimmest of husbands would smell a rat if he found official forms reminding his wife about compulsory sheep-dipping tucked behind the clock on the mantelpiece.

'And what about the smell?' I asked. 'You must have reeked of lanolin sometimes when you'd been handling the sheep.'

'The smell was never a problem,' said Barbara. 'I'd already been spinning for some time so there was often a sheepy smell. Anything extra can always be disguised by sloshing a bit of perfume about.'

'But what about the sheeps' own fleeces, apart from the smell? You can't hide twenty adult fleeces in your underwear drawer.'

'We've got a biggish house,' said Barbara. 'I rolled them up tight and put them in bags on the landing.'

'Cor,' I said, impressed. I couldn't imagine Brian navigating his way round twenty newly appeared lumps outside the bathroom. But Barbara's husband having been told that there were a few fleeces upstairs didn't investigate further, otherwise he would have put two and two together and found it made twenty. Obviously the secret of successful concealment is not to conceal everything.

One of the dodgiest moments Barbara had was when she and her husband were at a party and a friend came over and said 'Hi Barbara, how are all your sheep?' The husband heard and looked at Barbara questioningly. Quick as a flash Barbara turned the remark into a joke along the lines of: 'It does seem like a whole flock, doesn't it? All the paraphernalia of spinning and weaving . . .,' kicking her friend by way of a hint.

When the real flock gave birth Barbara had the almost unheard of good luck of trouble-free lambing. Her own good management must have been largely responsible but sometimes even the most conscientious stock-keepers have problems with animals. Barbara's flock of twenty became fifty and the dancing children on their visits home found themselves pressed into service. There were castrations to be done (very difficult from a textbook and best glossed over), extra hay to be humped, extra vigilance over the new lambs, and all this still a secret.

The lambs grew up and Barbara planned to upgrade the flock into milk sheep. There is a growing demand for milk ewes (as opposed to meat and wool sheep) to meet the needs of sheep cheese producers. Barbara started the breeding programme but before two years had passed the friend who was providing the grazing had to move house. This would have meant starting all over again with new grazing and as this was not at all easy to come by Barbara reluctantly decided to reduce the flock to a more manageable size. She advertised her ewes (all named and tame) and found good homes for all except a few she wanted to keep. These, together with the original two ponies and the goat, were transferred to another field where they all live as 'the pony' still.

What an amazing woman. It's only with the greatest difficulty that I manage to hide away Brian's Christmas presents, never mind 50 sheep, 2 ponies and a goat.

Chapter Three

DRIVING UP THE gravelled approach to a period house one morning (we mobile dog ladies get to see some jolly nice properties) I was ambushed by my customer, a middle-aged 'country smart' woman who nipped out from behind a tree and waved me down. I switched off the engine and she leaned in through the open window and whispered 'Leave your car here.' Experience has taught me there is usually a logical explanation for most strange requests so I got out quietly with my dog bag in one hand and a spanner in the other just in case.

We tiptoed past the front of the house where she made further shushing gestures and pointed up to the brickwork under the eaves. 'Wasps?' I mouthed.

'No, children. We try not to disturb them,' she whispered. Then, in a normal voice once we had got past the danger zone, 'Sorry about that. They broke up yesterday and I'm leaving them in bed as long as poss. Would you like some sherry?'

I nearly said what at eleven in the morning but thought better of it. I was already awash with indifferent coffee from the previous customer and sherry would make a welcome change. While she poured the drinks I unpacked my bag and made friends with the two spaniels who were the reason for my visit. They were rather woolly and she wanted them clipped right out except for their leg feathering. 'My husband likes to take them rabbiting in the evenings,' she explained. 'They come back so full of burrs it takes us hours to untangle them.'

'Mm it would,' I said. I attached a medium-fine blade onto the clippers and joked that they would look like a couple of skinheads for a few days. She didn't think that was funny so I shut up and got on with my work while she read the *Telegraph*. The dogs were well trained, the kitchen was farmhousey and cool and I had a large sherry to sip – altogether a very pleasing set up for a canine beautician.

Then the door opened and a boy of about fourteen slouched in. He was wearing torn jeans, a white T-shirt with the most obscene slogan I had ever seen and smelly plimsolls with more four-letter words. 'Oh good, you're dressed,' his mother said with forced brightness. The apparition withdrew and called up the stairs: 'Mum's drinking with some old bag. Whatja wanna eat?'

Before the mother could start apologising I said, 'Don't worry about it. At least he's not wearing earrings or nose studs.'

'That wasn't my son that was my daughter,' said the mother topping up her glass and sliding the sherry bottle over to me. 'And she did have earrings on last night. Swastikas. Simon too – he had swastikas.'

'Do they go to boarding school?' I asked.

'Oh yes. Quite strict ones. I suppose they have to let off steam in the holidays but it seems to get worse every term. Oh my God.' Another adolescent had materialised; this time it was unmistakably a boy – in swimming trunks and with aubergine-dyed hair. 'Good morning, Mother dear, what was that I heard about letting off steam?'

'Simon!'

'Mother?'

'You've *dyed your hair*.'

Idiot, I thought, you've played it all wrong. Now don't make things worse by saying wait-till-your-father-gets-home.

'I don't know what your father's going to say when he sees you,' said Simon's mother.

By the time I had finished the dogs Simon had lapsed into the same pseudo cockney as his sister and both children were filling the peaceful kitchen with noise and toast. 'It's only for six weeks,' I said trying to be helpful as I prepared to go.

'Eight,' said the mother gloomily. 'Anyway thank you for doing the dogs, they look lovely. I'll recommend you.'

'Thank you. Bye.'

*

She was as good as her word and recommended me to several other dog owners who also passed me on and so my doggy circle grew. It was in this way that I came to know Mr Lyle, a very shy man who communicated solely through his dog.

The first I knew about Mr Lyle's shyness was when the phone rang one day and a voice said: 'My name is Pedro Poodle and I would like to make an appointment for a clip, please.' Now it's not what I would call normal for dogs to make their own calls so I assumed that the owner's name was Mr Poodle. I entered the appointment in my diary, took down the address and then said: 'What breed of dog?'

'I'm a poodle. Black standard, six years old.'

'Right,' I said, a bit puzzled. 'See you on Friday then Mr, er, Poodle.'

When I told Brian I had been talking to a dog on the phone he said he wasn't surprised. Ever since Pierre Trudeau (a Yorkshire terrier) had bitten the milkman and been put on tranquillisers Brian had withdrawn into a fog of non-comprehension whenever I recounted the latest dog deed. He says I don't tell things in the right order and he may be right, but I think if he had been paying attention he would have known that the real Pierre Trudeau doesn't bite milkmen.

However, to return to the terribly shy Mr Lyle. I went to the house as arranged and the door was opened by a man and a black poodle. I looked at the man and told him who I was, but he, instead of replying directly, kept his eyes down on the dog and said good morning. At first I thought he might be blind because he didn't make any eye contact but as he led the way confidently through the house to the kitchen it was obvious he could see perfectly well.

'Nice day, isn't it, Mr – er.' Nothing like the weather for openers. 'Going to be hot again.'

'It's lovely,' agreed the man, 'but too hot for me in my thick woolly coat. I'll be glad to have it all clipped off. Shall I stand on the table or do you prefer to work on the floor?'

26

Before I knew quite how it had happened I found that I too was using Pedro as a go-between. It sounds tricky but once you get the hang of it it's not too difficult. I even – daringly I thought – asked Pedro if he read L.P. Hartley and Pedro said he never read novels but was keen on Roman history. An intellectual dog with an interest in archaeology, Pedro seemed decidedly short on humour. When I suggested that digging up bones sounded an ideal hobby for a dog he said scornfully: 'I don't dig up Roman *bones*. I'm not that sort of dog at all.' He told me his surname was Lyle, the same as his dad's. I was greatly relieved to hear it since I couldn't have brought myself to call the man Mr Poodle even if it had been his name. The only ticklish problem, literally, was when I came to Pedro's paws. Poodles grow thick matts of fur between the claws and these have to be clipped out regularly or the dog might develop eczema. Pedro told me that he disliked electric clippers on his feet and would prefer me to use scissors but by this time I was so confused by the Roman history and so forth I picked up the clippers by mistake. Pedro kept pulling his foot away and Mr Lyle, in the persona of the dog, kept laughing wildly. 'It tickles,' he chortled, 'I've got such ticklish paws. Please use the scissors.' His laughter set me off so there we were, Mr Lyle and I, doubled up while Pedro, the real owner of the ticklish feet, looked on disapprovingly.

That evening when I told Brian that I had had an entire clipping session with no direct human conversation he said Mr Lyle sounded barmy and that I shouldn't go again.

'He's not barmy,' I said indignantly, 'he's just paralysingly shy. Your Totnes lot are a sight barmier than Mr Lyle.' (The recent summer solstice had seen a mass migration from Totnes of would-be Druids who had come back even more into pantheism and meditation.)

'They're safely barmy,' Brian insisted. 'Your Mr Lyle could be a homicidal maniac for all you know.'

'You didn't say that about Mr Rosenberg.'

Brian roared with laughter and said Mr Rosenberg was hardly likely to murder me, quite the reverse. 'He gave you a fiver tip, didn't he?'

27

'Two pounds,' I said coldly.

Mr Rosenberg had an Airedale called Moses, a large dog who objected strenuously to being clipped. First we stood him on the floor but he had too much room to manoeuvre so we stood him on a table. He still had too much room so Mr Rosenberg fetched a narrow bench and we put him on that, sandwiched firmly between us. He struggled like mad but with two people restraining him he couldn't get away and I clipped the whole of one side without too much difficulty. Then we turned him round so that I could start on the other side and it suddenly occurred to Moses that maybe passive resistance would do the trick. He sagged limply so to get him to stand properly again I slid my hand under his chest and up the other side. Unfortunately it was hard to tell where Moses ended and Mr Rosenberg began and my hand came to rest up against Mr Rosenberg's lower front, to put it politely. I couldn't take it away or Mr Rosenberg would know that I knew so I left it there and clipped Moses with the other hand as fast as I could.

The episode needn't have been embarrassing. I should have said 'Oops sorry, Mr Rosenberg, I seem to be groping you' but not having been trained in Encounters of this kind I couldn't. Mr Rosenberg didn't seem to mind. He said 'My Moses is hard work, eh?'

'Yes he jolly well is,' I said. 'Let's put him on the floor and have a breather.' At last our enforced intimacy ended and we had a half time cup of coffee. Moses was even more uncooperative afterwards but I didn't fancy another grope (not that Mr Rosenberg wasn't fanciable) so I chained him to the leg of the kitchen table and finished the job on the floor. Mr Rosenberg gave me two pounds extra and said he hoped I hadn't been put off by such a big strong dog. Brian, needless to say, is still dining out on that one and for all I know so is Mr Rosenberg.

Miss Hughes was another unconventional person who enjoyed the same reclusive lifestyle as Mr Lyle. She wasn't a dog customer

28

but someone we met when househunting. From time to time she tired of her own company and would advertise her house for sale in order to meet new people. Not knowing that Miss Hughes had no intention of selling, Brian and I answered one of her adverts and went to view the house.

Before going in we walked round the outside of the house to get an idea of the layout. Then we opened the front gate and walked up the path. The front door opened a crack and a double barrel shotgun was levelled at our heads. 'If you're estate agents you can bugger off,' said a firm elderly voice.

'We're not estate agents,' we called, warming to someone who seemed prepared to do what most of us only dream about. 'We're prospective buyers.'

The gun was lowered and the door was opened by a woman of about eighty. We introduced ourselves and learned that she was Miss Hughes. She didn't apologise for the reception but casually parked the gun in the hall and invited us in. The house stank to high heaven as did Miss Hughes herself, dressed in an ensemble that looked like Cinderella on a bad day. She must have noticed us gasping for air because she said she had to keep all the windows closed to safeguard her valuables. We looked around for some valuables but as everything was inches thick in dust it was hard to tell a Chippendale chair from a Sainsbury's grocery box.

Miss Hughes saw us looking and laughed. 'It's not my furniture that's valuable it's my cars,' she said.

'Yes of course,' we said patronisingly, as though soothing a drunk. We followed her upstairs. Miss Hughes flung open a bedroom door with a flourish. 'My car,' she said proudly. And there in the bedroom in a very good condition was a baby Austin.

When we had recovered from the initial shock (oddly enough it was the bed and the chest of drawers that looked out of place) Brian said, 'How did you get the car into the bedroom, Miss Hughes?'

'Arnold brought it up in pieces.'

'Arnold?'

'My brother. You couldn't get petrol during the war so he laid up all his cars.'

Brian, visualising a car in each of the five bedrooms suddenly went off the boil as regards househunting. He said 'It's not quite what we're looking for, Miss Hughes. We won't take up any more of your time.'

But Miss Hughes wouldn't hear of us leaving. 'You must see the rest of the house,' she insisted. 'It's lovely and dry.' We could see by the rustless state of the Austin that it was indeed a house with no damp problems but the overpowering smell of neglect and B.O. was not conducive to a long visit. Brian asked if he could open some windows but Miss Hughes wouldn't let him in case burglars came after the car which she said had been made in 1923. It didn't seem to have occurred to her that stealing a car from a first floor bedroom would be beyond most housebreakers.

She showed us the other bedrooms, all chock full of junk. Basically it was a good sound house that could have been made very attractive after a mass clearance and fumigation. Brother Arnold had laid up his other cars in garages and sheds but as the grounds were almost completely overgrown with brambles we didn't look in. Poor Arnold had been killed in the war. Miss Hughes showed us his photograph together with four log-books and also, inexplicably, her own birth certificate which showed that she was eighty-six.

'You're asking an awful lot for the house, Miss Hughes,' Brian said. He was more cheerful now that he knew there were no more bedroom-based cars.

'How much money have you got?' countered Miss Hughes.

Over a cup of tea which we had the greatest difficulty in disposing of as there were no houseplants handy we realised that the 'House for Sale' advert had been no more than a lure. Several times Miss Hughes said 'I shall die here, I love this house,' which is terribly off-putting to people who are thinking of living there themselves. Also off-putting was her septic tank horror story. There are few country dwellers who don't have a septic tank horror story and personally I think all Dyno Rod operators

30

should receive automatic knighthoods, but Miss Hughes's was worse than most. After recounting it (with relish we realised later) she went on to tell us that the neighbours were a Bad Lot. They held wild drunken parties every Saturday night and threw empty beer bottles over the hedge onto her land.

After making us promise to come and visit her again (which we did) Miss Hughes let us go. We drove at once to the drunken neighbours' house half a mile away. A baby and a toddler were playing on the neat lawn in front of the house while their mother, a girl in her twenties, was unpegging some nappies from the washing line. We told her we were househunting in the area and had been to see Miss Hughes's house. The girl laughed and said we were the fourth couple in a fortnight. 'She's not really selling it, you know,' she said. 'If anyone shows any genuine interest she invents stories about us keeping killer dogs here and getting our boozy friends to pee in her garden.'

'How about beer bottles thrown over the hedge,' I said.

'No such luck. We couldn't afford the beer. Did you see the Alvis and the Lagonda?'

'We saw their log books. She's a very interesting old lady, isn't she?'

'She's a dear in her way. We try to keep a discreet eye on her but I must admit I'd feel happier if she didn't have that loaded gun by the door.'

'Oh surely it's not loaded,' said Brian.

'Not loaded? I'll say it's loaded. Try walking up the path in a suit and carrying a briefcase.'

When I told my mother about Miss Hughes she said the smell in the house was probably rotting estate agents and asked if she could come with us next time we paid a social call. 'With a name like Hughes she must be Welsh,' she said.

'So? Do all your woad-covered cousins bury estate agents under the floorboards?'

'Nothing so crude,' said Anne. She had been brought up in a part of rural Wales where people took a dim view of the orthodox legal system and would spend the long winter evenings plotting revenge against those who had wronged them.

31

Mostly the wrongdoers found themselves on the receiving end of a simple spell or two (much cheaper than a solicitor) but in a couple of cases that my mother recalled the victims were done away with permanently.

There was one young woman, married to a drunk who beat her, who devised and carried out the perfect murder. With great patience she taught her three-year-old son how to shoot an air rifle accurately, rewarding him with sweets whenever he hit a cardboard target. The infant was then tried out with a twelve-bore which the mother propped up for him on the kitchen table. He practised 'Bang bang you're dead' until he was bullseye perfect.

One evening the husband reeled in, stood conveniently framed in the doorway for a moment, and was shot dead by his trigger-happy son. At the inquest everyone said how dangerous it was to leave loaded guns within reach of toddlers and after a bit of tut tutting, sympathy was extended to the grieving widow and that was the end of the matter.

Another bad character came to a sticky end (forensic details unknown) and on this occasion the entire community closed ranks, covering up the crime and the body in a most imaginative way. The murder took place in April which is a good month for murder as the earth is soft by then. By the time the local police had given up and called in the Yard every cottager and small-holder for miles was displaying a freshly dug vegetable garden. So keen were these gardeners to start their growing season they had even planted out their runner beans. Salad crops were in, and potatoes and carrots, and everywhere there was black cotton stretched tight across the soil to discourage birds. The policemen scrabbled away rather half-heartedly here and there (in those days they didn't have the sophisticated detecting equipment they have now) and the villagers looked on, Celtic tempers rising. It would have taken a brave squad to dig up everyone's plot and if there was one place where the new growth was extra lush, Plod of the Yard didn't spot it; they all went away leaving the crime unsolved.

Personally I blame the absence of television for all that

inner-village crime. Old people often say 'We made our own entertainments in those days' as if it was necessarily a good thing but was it? If they had had television in that village (which was far from unique) their vengeances could have taken the form of compulsory soap-opera viewing for their victims. Admittedly a sort of brain death but at least it would have been legal.

Chapter Four

IN THE AUTUMN a number of green laners left to go to university and were replaced by some youngsters with the same curious attitude to timekeeping as the old-stagers, the Filberts and Bees. Nine to five was a concept totally beyond their grasp. They would arrive for work at any time from 10 a.m. onwards and would start to get homesick at 4 p.m. It wasn't that they didn't enjoy the work it was just that they didn't like sacrificing so much leisure time to do it in.

For some weeks they had been driven by Brian in one of the old bangers when out of the blue there was a mutiny. Someone could smell carbon monoxide. Brian stopped the minibus and they all scrambled out and went home. (They had a great homing instinct, any trouble and off they would go.) Brian took the bus back to the garage for a checkup and to everyone's horror the exhaust system *was* found to be faulty. Carbon monoxide was leaking into the interior and had been for some time. Brian's window on the driver's side had never closed properly so he hadn't been affected by the fumes but the others could have been gassed.

'We *told* you we sensed something was wrong,' they said triumphantly when they showed up for work the following day. 'We haven't felt right for weeks.' Brian said that as the symptoms of gas poisoning were identical to those of a mantra-induced trance – the youngsters liked to meditate as they travelled – how was he supposed to know what was going on in the back?

After this incident the green laners were more than ever convinced that work was a perilous occupation and took to having extra long lunch hours to keep their courage up. Sometimes if it was raining they would go to a pub but normally they had sandwiches in the green lane where they happened to be at the time. Sitting quietly in the shade of a tree inevitably led to minute observations of the flora and fauna around them which was precisely what they were being paid to do. Brian never had the heart to explain the mechanics of a working lunch.

An idyllic life, but not without its hiccups. A few al fresco lunches later one of the female members of the group complained to the management that she was a victim of sexual harassment. Sadly this turned out to be a case of wishful thinking. In order to be harassed sexually it's fairly important for the victim to be recognisably male or female and in this girl's case nobody ever knew she was a girl until she went to have a pee behind a hedge. Filbert was already there for the same reason and the girl was upset because he just carried on.

When Brian came home and told me the tale I naturally thought that either they'd all been at the funny fags or that Brian had nosedived into early senility. 'Not noticed that it was female?' I said incredulously.

'No.'

'But she must have a name?'

'She's called Six.'

'Ah.' The self-chosen names of the alternative people were always a challenge. After some months' practice we were getting quite good at unravelling the reasons behind the choices. 'Six being her lucky cosmic number? Something like that?'

'Not even warm. I'll give you a clue – it's an abbreviation.'

Six, I thought. That's vi. Something beginning with vi. Vinegar? Vitamin? Surely even an alternative parent wouldn't call a baby Vitamin. 'I give up.'

'It's Viola,' said Brian, 'But she didn't like being called Vi so she called herself Six.'

'Right, fair enough. The name doesn't tell you anything but what does she look like?'

'Like a commando. Cropped hair, combat gear and Doc Martens. Poor old Fil had quite a shock when she screamed at him.'

35

'And did she really complain to the boss later?'

'Yes. Then the boss found out that she'd left her four previous jobs because of alleged sexual harassment so he told her to shut up and grow up.'

The next day Six took her strange battle to a higher authority. This time she complained that the boss himself had sexually harassed her in his office at 9 a.m. As she hadn't actually got to work until 10.30 her story lacked a certain something and she was asked if she wouldn't prefer to seek employment elsewhere. So after just two days as a green laner she left to become a fish gutter in Iceland where it was rumoured you could earn £200 a week.

While Brian and co. continued to explore Devon's countryside I was becoming something of a connoisseur of old Hollywood films. This came about because being a travelling dog groomer I was frequently in somebody else's house during the afternoon and it's then that they show old films on television. The people who watch films in the afternoon are the bored, the old and the sick. Discounting the bored, whom I never met (it would be hard to be bored with a dog around), many of my customers were housewives with a bedbound parent in a downstairs room. As winter progressed it seemed as though all the pensioners in Devon had had falls of some sort and were convalescing with married daughters. And if they hadn't got broken limbs they were incapacitated in other ways – bereaved maybe, or bronchitic, or just plain old and waiting to die in the comfort of a family home with the TV on full blast. One such household was the McDougalls'.

Thanks to the foresight of whoever designed the poodle, dog ladies are assured of an all-year income. Other breeds only need an occasional trim but the poodle coat is fast growing and needs attention every six to eight weeks. Toffee McDougall was a poodle, a brown standard who lived with his very nice family near Paignton and who had his hair cut regularly. Mrs McDougall phoned one day to book me for 'Toffee's usual' and told me to let myself in as she would be out having her own hair cut that afternoon. I asked her why she always had her hair done on the same day as Toffee and she said it was because her husband made such a fuss of the freshly turned out Toffee it made her jealous. 'Well really,' I said, 'it's come to something when you have to compete with the dog.'

'It certainly has,' she said. 'Time was when he'd come through the door and start hugging and kissing me. Now he walks past me and puts his arms round Toffee. By the way we've got Grandad in the chair downstairs with his chest. Would you make him a cup of tea if he wants one? Ta. The key's under the geranium.'

When the appointed day came I copied out my list of customers together with the words 'hen pen' (which is still a mystery) against a two o'clock appointment and 'geranium Grandad' against Toffee McDougall. It wasn't until I arrived at the McDougall house that I thought what geranium? Even in the tropics of Paignton, February is not the season for geraniums. After some thought I figured that the key would be under where Mrs McDougall's favourite geranium *had* been last summer. It was, so I let myself in and a man's voice said 'I've waited all these years to hold you tight.' It wasn't the husband eager for a bit on the side but one of the old films on television turned up so loudly that even Toffee hadn't heard me come in. He was asleep in his basket next to a radiator and when he did see me he reacted the same as most of my hairy customers – oh my Dog not *her* again. Closing his eyes quickly he buried his face in his flank hoping that if he couldn't see me I couldn't see him. The actors in the film were struggling with a cliché-laden script and had now been joined by an orchestra. Following the deafening sound to its source I went into the sitting room and found Grandad asleep in an armchair with the TV remote control still clutched in his hand. I woke him carefully, took the gadget from him and turned the volume down. Grandad glared crossly at the television screen and said 'What's the score?'

'It's not football,' I said, although the passionate clinch in close up could well have been Lineker being rewarded by an affectionate winger. 'It's a film.'

'What happened to the match then?'

'That was Sunday. It's Thursday today. Would you like a cup of tea?'

'Aye I would. You the nurse?'

I explained who I was but it was like Brian trying to explain punctuality to the Totnes-ites. The old man thought I was pulling his leg. Dogs having their own special barber calling at the house, whatever next? In fact he got quite breathless laughing at the idea so it seemed safer to let him go on thinking I was the nurse. As I was leaving the room to put the kettle on he said 'The lassie's daft to trust him.'

'Who?'

He pointed to the television. 'Daft,' he repeated. 'He's got white shoes on. Never trust a bugger in white shoes.'

The lassie in the film was trusting the white-shod man with everything the censor permitted and you could tell by the music that she was making a Big Mistake. 'Get shot of him lass,' Grandad shouted. He thumped his fist on the remote control which I had foolishly put down on the arm of his chair and suddenly there was Mavis Nicholson interviewing some people against a backdrop which looked spartan after the expensive Hollywood set. Although Grandad had been so very perceptive about the white shoes he failed to notice the lack of continuity and was still happily engrossed in the Mavis Nicholson programme when I brought the tea in.

A martyred looking Toffee was coaxed out of his basket and I was just finishing clipping him when Mrs McDougall came home.

'Sorry I'm late,' she said. 'I had to fetch Janet from school and we got caught in the traffic.' Janet was a lively seven-year-old who answered to 'you holy terror' and 'Grandad's little popsy'. She flung herself at Toffee as though they had been separated for months and some of my tools went flying. Mrs McDougall said, 'If you break anything, Janet, you'll get a smack.'

'Miss Gibbs doesn't believe in corporal punishment,' said Janet.

'Miss Gibbs knocks off at half-past three,' said her mother crisply. 'Now go and keep Grandad company while I get your tea ready.' Janet zoomed out of the kitchen only to reappear a moment later to say Grandad wanted a sausage sandwich and could she have a sausage sandwich too.

'You're both having haddock and poached eggs,' said Mrs McDougall, 'so let me get on. Go and watch television.' As soon as Janet had gone she said, 'Oh dear, I shouldn't have said that. Not on a Thursday.'

'A grave error,' I agreed and smiled complacently to myself. As every mother, foster mother or child-minder knows, Thursdays and Mondays are *Blue Peter* days – 'glue days' some people call them. For the uninitiated I should explain that *Blue Peter* is a children's TV programme unrivalled in excellence. It stimulates, educates and entertains. It keeps its several million young viewers anchored in one place for a whole half hour twice a week. Part of its appeal to the children (but not their mothers) is the way it demonstrates model making. A presenter will assemble some common-place household items and with a few deft movements and one or two dabs of glue will show how easy it is to construct, say, dolls' furniture or a Christmas present for a luckless parent. Then the programme finishes and the BBC staff go home leaving millions of mothers tearing their hair out while their offspring strip the house like soldier ants of any object which looks suitable for glueing to any other object. By the time the husband gets home from work there will be enough materials on the kitchen table to build a house extension, the child or children will have blissfully glued themselves and everything else to the chairs and the mother will be downing neat whisky.

'It's all right for you to smirk,' Mrs McDougall said. 'Your kids are grown up, aren't they?'

'I did an extended tour of duty,' I boasted, and told her how Brian and I had often had twenty small children in the house, all *Blue Peter* fans.* She was clearly impressed.

'I can see why you took to dogs,' she said. 'I mean, even if they bite you or play up, they must be a better bet than double-sided sellotape twice a week.'

---

* See *The Year of the Cornflake* and *Green Behind the Ears*.

I said I didn't know any *adults* who could master double-sided sellotape, let alone children. We compared notes on glueing techniques and discovered that neither of us knew the difference between a collage and a montage. Rather than bother looking up the words in a dictionary Mrs McDougall called out to Janet, 'What's a montage, love?'

Grandad yelled back, 'No she doesn't and neither do I. We want sausage sandwiches.' Janet ran in and said they weren't doing montages that day, they were doing bird cooking and could she have a basin and some peanuts. Her headlong rush scattered the neat heap of Toffee's fur which I was about to put in the bin. Janet 'helped' to pick it up. Toffee helped too and Mrs McDougall looked hopefully at the kitchen clock to see how long it was to Janet's bedtime. I went home.

One of the most interesting people I met through dog-clipping was Harry, the man who sold his wife. He was one of my regular customers until he moved to Ireland. He lived with a gorgeous shaggy black mongrel called Robert and an awful nagging wife called Christine. I've never seen a man as henpecked as Harry. He was a recently retired fireman so he was physically tough but it needed more than toughness to withstand Christine's tongue. She was big with it, eighteen stone of solid fishwife, a horrible woman with horrible naggy friends like herself. Whenever I went to the house to clip Robert she would either be 'doing the chores' (a lot of mat shaking and mop wringing) or talking about the chores to her coffee morning coven. Harry and I would take Robert to the garden shed, dog clipping being considered too mucky an occupation for a decent woman's kitchen. The shed was lovely. Harry had made a real sanctuary there for himself with fish tanks and some cages for his many furred and feathered pets. It smelt of creosote and sawdust and Harry's pipe which was another thing banned in the house.

Christine had religious mania which didn't exactly add to her charms, and had put God adverts all over the walls. After the King's Cross fire disaster, Harry, who had spent twenty years as a fireman and was deeply affected by the tragedy, took down the 'God Cares' posters and threw them away. It was a bad move. Christine intensified her nagging until Harry grew so withdrawn it looked as though he might have a breakdown.

Then one day everything had changed. I went to the house to clip Robert and was about to go to the back door when I saw Harry standing at the front gate smiling broadly. 'You can come in this way today,' he said. 'I've got rid of Christine.' My mind must have been on the Welsh village murders because I immediately assumed he meant he had killed her. 'How?' I said, meaning with an axe or pushed under a bus.

'I sold her.'

I stopped halfway up the garden path and stared at him. 'You sold Christine? But who on *earth* would want her?'

'Come indoors, don't want half the village knowing our business, eh Robert?' Harry and Robert led the way through the hall and into the kitchen. Harry put the kettle on and I took stock of the transformation in the room. Christine's worktops were now covered in bird cages while on the floor was an open hutch with a couple of rather pongy ferrets gnawing at a piece of log. I said politely that it looked much more homely although to be honest I don't really like the smell of ferrets and Harry said it was good for the animals to have a change of scene. He knew I was dying to hear about the sale of Christine and deliberately kept me in suspense until the tea was poured out. 'Come on,' I said. 'Spill the beans. Have you been reading Thomas Hardy?'

'Who's Thomas Hardy?'

'He was a writer. One of his books was about a man who sold his wife.'

'Did he now?' Harry seemed a bit crestfallen that he wasn't after all the trendsetter in this field. 'How much did he get for her?'

'I don't remember.'

'I got thirty-six thousand pounds for Christine.'

Some of my tea went down the wrong way and Harry thumped me on the back. 'There, that surprised you, didn't it? Don't suppose your Thomas Hardy got that much.'

'Definitely not. Are you going to tell me who bought Christine or are you sworn to secrecy?'

'It's a chap called Paul. Daft sod.' Harry lit his pipe and puffed clouds of hitherto forbidden smoke into the air. 'He's a widower; I suppose I mustn't call him a daft sod seeing he's doing me a big favour, but that's what he is. He's in Christine's church and they've been going to evening meetings together for some time.'

'Have they been having an affair?'

'Shouldn't think so. I don't imagine he's that daft. He says he admires a woman who knows her own mind. Anyway, he and some of the other church members were holding one of their pow wows here a couple of months back – they have a rota for meetings in each others' houses – and Paul came out into the garden for a smoke' – Harry paused to make the point that even Christine's man of the moment wasn't allowed to smoke in the house – 'and we got talking.'

'You being banished to the shed as usual? Go on.'

'Well, it seems that Paul and his late wife had always liked this house but when it was up for sale, before we bought it, Paul couldn't afford it. He said what a lucky fellow I was (he talks like that) to have such a nice home and a good wife and what wouldn't he give to be in my shoes.'

'So you said make me an offer?'

'Not straight off I didn't. You know how it is when you go fishing? You get a nibble but you don't strike too soon in case the fish comes off the hook?'

'Harry,' I said admiringly, 'you are amazing.'

'I'm patient,' said Harry and went on to tell me how he had worked, first on Paul then on Christine, singing the praises of one to the other and making sure that they spent plenty of time together. All this had taken several weeks, during which time Harry and Robert had stayed out, walking until dark sometimes, to make sure that Paul was getting to feel thoroughly at home in the house. Then he had struck. He told Christine that he wanted a divorce. In previous years whenever he had mentioned divorce Christine, in the time-honoured way of bullies, had threatened to kill herself. But this time surprise surprise, she ran to Paul for comfort. Paul confronted Harry and rather half-heartedly called him a bounder. Harry admitted to being a bounder and offered to sell Paul the house for thirty-six thousand pounds on condition that Paul took care of Christine.

'But Harry,' I interrupted, 'the house is worth much more than that.'

'Not with her in it it's not. I'd have sold it to him for ten thousand but he didn't even try to bargain.'

'You won't get much of a house for yourself for thirty-six thousand,' I said, trying not to sound like the nagging Christine. But to my surprise Harry produced newspapers with adverts for houses from as little as £6000. Quite nice places too, three up two down and with a few acres.

'They're in southern Ireland,' said Harry. 'I've decided to get as far away as possible in case she changes her mind.'

'I'm very pleased for you,' I said. 'It'll be lovely for Robert to have a place in the country.'

'I'll buy him a pup for company when we're settled,' said Harry. 'And I'd ask you to come with us if you weren't already spoken for. You're good with animals.'

I wasn't sure if he was offering marriage or a job as head zoo keeper but it was nice to be asked and I said I would bear it in mind if ever Brian decided to sell me. Soon afterwards Harry and Robert moved to Ireland and sent us a postcard: 'From Harry, Robert, Kathleen and Moira.' It sounded to me as though Harry had wasted no time in finding girlfriends for himself and Robert but Brian thought Kathleen and Moira may have been the ferrets.

Chapter Five

PART OF THE point of the green lanes project was to educate, and to this end the field-workers would be invited to local primary schools to talk to the children about the origins of green lanes. The boss would pair them off for this job, issue them with 'props' (which I'll come to in a minute) and throw them to the seven-year-olds.

When it was Brian's turn to do a school stint he was relieved to find himself paired with Joe, a lad in his twenties who didn't have a Mohican haircut and didn't spend all day trying to find the meaning of life. The straighter members of the workforce had recently had rather a fraught time with Filbert and a new girl called Lettice. Filbert, who couldn't spell, had fallen in love with the green-ness of her name and had set his heart on convincing her they were made for each other. The trouble was that Lettice didn't view Filbert in quite the same light. She was a normal, rather upper-crust girl who was hoping to read botany at Oxford if she got good A levels, and she couldn't see that life in a squat with Filbert had a lot to offer by comparison.

Brian and Joe were glad to have a day away from the lovesick Filbert. Arriving at the school they were welcomed by the children's class teacher and taken in to meet their young audience. Joe had done school visits before so he took charge. First he introduced himself and Brian and told the children that there was no need for them to be called Sir but just plain Joe and Brian. (One little boy got a bit confused and called them Sir Joe and Sir Brian for the rest of the day.) Next he talked about the history of green lanes, how animals had worn tracks through the undergrowth, and how man in pre-medieval times had followed in those same tracks year after year until the routes were recognisably small narrow paths. After that, said Joe, our ancestors had made fields, banking up the earth all round to stop their animals from getting out. What grew in the new earth banks was what had been growing in the ground, and is still there now, hundreds of years later. Ignoring enquiries about why everything hadn't gone bad if it was so old, Joe continued the story of the evolution of lanes. Farmworkers going to and from work along the same daily routes between the newly constructed earth banks, trod the ground into hard-packed surfaces and so the lanes were born.

The teaching programme was broken up into three periods. This was ostensibly to allow for the relatively short attention span of seven-year-olds but after hearing Brian's account of the school visit I concluded that it was also to allow him and Joe to recover between sessions, like boxers. After the talk Joe invited questions. These ranged from 'What is an ancestor?' and 'What is a medieval?' to 'Where did you buy your trainers, Joe?' Brian was asked if his daddy had been a peasant in the Middle Ages and when he said no, his daddy had worked for the Gas Board the children thought he was joking.

The next part of the lesson was in the form of a play written by Joe. Some of the children were lined up to portray a hedge, their props for this exacting role being bamboo rods on which were fastened painted lengths of sacking. Half of the rest of the children donned animal masks and the other half dressed up as milkmaids, serfs and other members of the peasantry. The play started.

Mice, moles and weasels scurried along the bottom of the hedge which broke ranks from time to time since no self-respecting small boy was going to be a boring old hedge when he was holding the perfect weapon to bash his enemies with. Then came the agricultural workers, plodding their weary way backwards and forwards for two or three hundred years, in the tracks made by the hedgerow creatures. Brian, as assistant stage manager, was supposed to see that all the children understood the historical sequence of events, and that the hedge evolved slowly as time passed. Fat chance. He was kept so busy separating mice locked in mortal combat and retrieving fox masks from the top of tall trees (the tall trees should have been saplings but they would keep standing up) that the play unfolded more haphazardly than planned.

The class teacher took charge of the children during the lunch hour and handed them back, refreshed, to Brian and Joe for the afternoon session. This was nature study or field-work as it's known nowadays and was held in a real green lane near the school.

'It's a sort of treasure hunt,' explained Joe, and Brian, who was not without experience of treasure hunts added firmly that there was to be no fighting and no crying. Joe continued: 'We want you to find as many different examples as you can of plants and insects. Each of you will have a questionnaire to fill in. When you think you've identified something look it up on your form and put a tick in the box next to the picture. If you're not sure what you've found bring it to us and we'll help you.' Before long the children were bringing beer cans, used condoms and cigarette packets and Brian and Joe had to explain the lifestyle of medieval peasants all over again. Somehow the Black Death found its way into what should have been a nature study and two of the boys hopped around pretending to be plague-carrying fleas. They were extremely noisy fleas especially when they landed on the still fighting mice, but thanks to the umpiring skills of Brian and Joe everyone managed to fill in their question-naires by the end of the afternoon. Then they all trooped back to school laden with 'specimens' for further study – wood lice, earwigs, an iron bar and countless caterpillars.

When Brian came home he was so tired after his back-to-school day he couldn't remember the word caterpillar. Clicking his fingers in annoyance as the word eluded him he said, 'You know the things I mean – butterflies' children.' This went straight in to our everyday vocabulary and we still call caterpillars 'butterflies' children'.

A few days after the school trip Joe and Brian received thank-you letters from the children. Seldom can bread and butter letters have been so lovingly composed or so appreciated. Here are some extracts: Dear Joe and Brian, you were ace . . .

Der Joe and Brin, thank you for takin us owt it were the nissest leson I had . . . Dear Brian and Darling Joe, we love you and Joes trainers were great . . . Dere Brian You were ACE Brian You were ACE . . . To Joe we found more WOOD LICE you showed us how to notis more lots of hugs xxx . . . Dearest Joe my favourite but I love Brin to . . . To Joe the greatest . . . Ace lesson Brian come and see us soon . . .

Drawings accompanied the letters, most depicting the green lane outing as a kind of Garden of Eden with Brian and Joe as Adam and Adam striding through the greenery. Some had seen it more as a game reserve; woodland mammals disproportionately large lay stealthily in wait to pounce on the smaller creatures. 'Our aynshint ansisters' were much in evidence too, staggering drunkenly up and down the lanes. True to their Blue Peter training the children had labelled everything in the pictures neatly and had printed their name, age and address on the backs of their work. Joe and Brian were thrilled to bits to get the letters and would have liked to keep them but the boss wanted them for the green lane records.

My own aynshint ansister liked to hear Brian's descriptions of Totnes. 'It sounds like my cup of tea,' she said, 'casual and historic at the same time. Can we go and have a look round one day?'

We didn't recognise the danger signals. After all, she'd only been in her present house a year – a comfortable semi with glorious views over the River Exe. We saw no risk in taking her to see Totnes.

After parking the car we strolled up the High Street, a short stretch of road containing as well as all the usual shops, no fewer than five bookshops. It may have been the bookshops that did it or the combination of bookshops and alternative people (some carrying the most adorable alternative babies in canvas slings) but by the time we had reached the middle of town Anne was hooked. She vanished into an estate agent's. Brian slumped onto the church wall.

'She may be just looking,' I said without much conviction.

We waited a while and then followed Anne into the estate agent's where a disconcerted assistant was trying to take down some particulars. 'There's Inky and Melly,' Anne was saying.

'Dogs,' put in Brian.

'And Bodie and Bumble.'

'More dogs?' said the assistant.

'Cats,' I said.

'This is my daughter,' said Anne and, before I could stop her, 'She writes books. Very good they are, all about . . .'

As I tend towards grievous bodily harm on these embarrassing occasions I went outside to wait on the church wall. When the others came out Anne handed me a sheet of house particulars. 'That's the one I want,' she said.

'You can't say that,' Brian protested. 'You really can't just buy the first house that you see without looking at lots beforehand.'

'Yes I can,' said Anne. Melly squatted in the gutter and made a small puddle. When she had finished a horrid old man who was also sitting on the church wall glared at Anne and said something about dogs being a threat to health. 'Oh yes I *do* agree with you,' said Anne. 'Why don't you phone the fire brigade? Tell them there's a tide of dog pee flooding down the street. Tell them to bring pumps before everyone drowns in it. Tell them—' The old man shuffled off and Anne, well pleased with her debut into Totnes society, said 'Let's go and buy me a house.'

She bought the first one she saw (we didn't even look at any others) and a few weeks later was a Totnes-ite. Her moving day nearly killed us because she hadn't thought to tell the removal firm that there was no road access to the house. They sent three men instead of six so Brian and I had to be three removal men for a day. By ten p.m. we were still ferrying and after it was all finished we literally couldn't stand up and went home locked in crouched positions like two question marks.

Among its many advantages Totnes (as far as I know) has no vandals. The young bloods are far too busy helping old

48

ladies across the road and studying the Karmic consequences of their actions to go in for mindless violence. Shortly after Anne's move she wanted something smashed up and whereas in most towns you can just put things outside the front gate and know that they'll either be stolen or broken up, this doesn't happen in Totnes. 'Why is it', said Anne crossly 'that you can never find a vandal when you want one?'

It is possible, of course, that when the alternative babies grow up there may be a pendulum swing back to conformity. We saw a small example of this recently. A very hippie mother clad in the tribal uniform of sacking and green wellies was queuing up at the greengrocers. With her was her son, a pale boy of about thirteen in grey flannels and a slogan-free shirt. The mother picked out a bunch of cut flowers and put it in her basket with the vegetables. The boy looked at the flowers anxiously and said, 'Mum, can we afford them . . .?'

His mother sighed with exasperation and said, 'Oh do stop being so *sensible*, Taurus.' Poor Taurus looked uncomfortable and it was hard not to feel a bit sorry for him even though my own sympathies will always lie with people who regard flowers as an essential part of the weekly shopping. What *is* going to be funny though is when the Tauruses and Merlins and Rainbows grow up and become the Mr and Mrs Borings of tomorrow. They'll all have to change their names just as their parents did only this time it will be back to Nigel and Darren and Marlene.

One person who was very pleased to have a grandmother living at the acknowledged centre of the New Age world was globe-trotting Marcus, now in his third year of non-stop travel. He had started out to hitch-hike round India but having done that he liked it so much he did it again. After the second circuit he found it impossible to break the habit and had since branched out to Burma, China, Tibet and Thailand. It was interesting to learn that there were hundreds and hundreds of similar youngsters travelling the world more or less permanently. They have to take short breaks occasionally to earn the money to continue travelling.

We had seen Marcus once, briefly one Christmas when we were living on Dartmoor. It was so cold for him after India that he simply couldn't get warm. He spent ten days alternately digging the garden and chopping wood in an attempt to stop his blood freezing. After there was no more wood left to chop he caught the first plane back to Delhi and was soon sending pictures of his beloved beach in Goa where the sand was as soft as talcum powder. His accommodation cost him 35p a day. 'That's marvellous,' he wrote, on hearing of Anne's move. 'Totnes is where it's at,' (something familiar about that?) and went on to ask if we'd heard the rumour that a new Messiah was due at Buckfast Abbey.

'Brian,' I said when he came in to look at the post. 'Did you know a new Messiah is due at Buckfast Abbey?'

'What do you mean due?' said Brian pedantically. 'Messiahs aren't trains.'

'It'll put property prices up.'

'This is a ridiculous conversation,' said Brian. 'Let me see Marcus's letter. While he read it I wondered if property prices in Jerusalem had been affected in AD 01. Since I don't believe that J.C. was ever more than a gifted young healer with rather confused ideas about his paternity, I hadn't taken much interest in that period of history. Pigs, I knew were considered a health hazard, rightly so in those days before the discovery of anthelmintics, but property was a closed book.

'If there *is* going to be a Messiah,' I persisted, 'we should buy a field near the abbey and rent out bits of it to newspaper reporters.'

Brian said that was propheteering (joke) and was the yuckiest idea I'd ever come up with and that anyway reporters stayed in hotels not tents. He flatly refused to believe in the Messiah prediction because he hadn't heard anything about it on the radio. (I think it's going to come as quite a shock to him when some cretin presses the nuclear button and blows us all to smithereens without having the courtesy to inform Radio 4 first.)

It did seem extraordinary though that youngsters on a beach thousands of miles away should be discussing something happening on our own doorstep, or rather something allegedly about to happen. I asked Brian to ask his workmates if anyone had come across a Messiah but when he did, *all* the self-discoverers claimed to know one. The area around Buckfast Abbey was stiff with Messiahs. I had to write back to Marcus for more details. Was his one the retired builder who charmed warts or the two-year-old godlet deliberately conceived at Stonehenge when his parents' planets were in the right position? The postal service to and from India is bullock-cart slow and by the time Marcus wrote again he was heading for Nepal and had lost interest in Buckfast Abbey. However, land prices in the area are rising even faster than they are everywhere else so maybe Marcus will get his scoop one of these days.

'After Nepal, Nobby and I are going to Japan,' he wrote, and we had to hunt back through his letters to remind ourselves who Nobby was. Marcus met so many new people it was impossible to keep up to date. Eventually we found Nobby in a photograph taken on the beach at Goa – a Japanese lad sandwiched between Marcus and a tall Kenyan called John, the three of them looking for all the world like the three boys in *Coral Island* – Ralph, Jack and Peterkin. 'We share the rent of this hut,' Marcus had written on the back of the snap. The hut was palm-fronded with a wooden verandah facing the sea and the rent was 60p a week. In order to continue to afford such a lavish lifestyle the boys had decided to go abroad for a while, earn some money and then regroup back at the hut later in the year.

John the Kenyan went off to Australia while Marcus and Nobby headed for Japan. Here they split up; Nobby to an unknown destination and Marcus in a borrowed suit to Tokyo. With forged references supplied by some of Nobby's friends (alternative Japanese – the movement is catching on) he got a well-paid job teaching English in a language school. 'Send my *Roget's Thesaurus*,' came one anguished letter, 'I've got to teach the other teachers how to teach.' It turned out that some of the other 'teachers' were German students who were working their passage round the world. They too had forged their own references but had come slightly unstuck when confronted by their classes. Marcus said he had to keep well out of earshot when the Germans were giving English lessons because he would end up with tears of laughter running down his face and that would have given the game away. The Japanese businessmen learning English from the Germans developed a quite incomprehensible pronunciation and naturally put their verbs at the end of sentences. This didn't matter too much in conversation classes but as Marcus said it won't do a lot for their export businesses if they write: 'I am your spare parts vaitink. With much haste I your nuts and bolts hunger for.'

As the cost of living in Tokyo is probably the highest in the world and as Marcus sees himself as something of a budget evangelist he rose to the challenge. From his relatively cheap 'Geijing' or guest house (five pounds a night exclusive of food) he explored Tokyo on foot and by bus and train, painstakingly noting down bargains. For instance, an organised coach tour of the city costs between £40 and £80 but Marcus's do-it-yourself tour cost him 50p – the price of a platform ticket on the main line train. Eating out was prohibitively expensive too (up to four pounds for a cup of coffee) so our hardworking sleuth unearthed several other options, from buying groceries and preparing packed meals in the guest-house to dining off free samples in department stores. 'It's funny,' wrote Marcus, 'to have all the shop assistants bowing and saying hello and thanking you endlessly for no apparent reason. They *like* you to try all the samples on display and when you've eaten everything up they refill the dishes and you start again if you're still hungry.'

After working in Tokyo for a few weeks he had saved enough money to live in India for another year. En route back to Goa he stopped off in Burma for ten days, which is all they allow tourists, and while he was there he hired a typewriter for 12p and wrote an article which he called 'The Budget Travellers' Guide to Tokyo'. His researches had been quite thorough and the article was packed with detailed information (including telephone numbers of guest-houses which carried the Marcus Seal of Approval) on how to have an interesting holiday in Tokyo without going bankrupt. His typing was terrible and the paper from Burma looked as though it had been made out of bleached rhubarb leaves but the content looked definitely saleable. We had the rhubarb leaves professionally transformed into fifteen pages of immaculate typescript and submitted the article to two magazines. Both turned it down, one saying it was not detailed enough and the other implying that *their* readers had plenty of money to spend on holidays. Marcus, who had never had anything rejected before – even his Disgusted of Tunbridge Wells letters to newspapers always got printed – was furious and accused me of watering down his deathless prose. As all I had actually done was remove a few adjectives and shorten some of his Levin-length sentences to manageable size, I sulked, which is not easy by letter. His masterpiece is still with us, in a cupboard, waiting to be discovered by a passing editor.

Chapter Six

MY FRIEND VIVIENNE, a cat expert, has a theory that you can tell a lot about a person by the sort of cat he or she chooses. Leaving aside the fact that most of us don't choose cats but have cats thrust upon us (it'll have to be put to sleep, Mummy, if they can't find it a good home) Viv was writing a book, part of which described owner/cat combinations. It seems that white cats are preferred by certain types of people, Siamese by other types and so on. According to Viv, cats, like dreams, reflect part of our unconscious minds. (She lives just outside Totnes but it's rubbed off on her.) For instance, if a person has delusions of grandeur or a streak of repressed violence their choice of cat is actually an unconscious statement about these ills. I've never understood why psychology always demands that things have to symbolise other things. It all sounds so unnecessarily complicated but Viv is brainier than I am so I expect she's right.

Although we hadn't chosen either of our cats we were pleased to learn that black and white cats symbolised humour and tabbies security. A bit dull but better dull than revealing repressed violence, not that Brian ever represses violence if he catches the cats digging up his seedlings. Assuming that the theory was correct, that cats' colour and breed do reflect the hidden bits of their owners, I wondered if it could be made to work in reverse. Could you calm down your neurotic friends by showering them with tabby kittens, or liven up dull men with ginger toms? No, said Viv firmly, cats are not antibiotics. Her book, which at that time was still not quite finished, was drafted to include a short chapter on the psychology of dogs and their owners. After some discussion we all felt that dog psychology was such a big subject it couldn't possibly be squeezed in at the end of a cat book, so Viv said she would finish the cat book then write a separate one about dogs. In the meantime I promised to pay closer attention to my dog customers and report back to Viv if I came across any examples of deviant behaviour which she could use.

With missionary zeal I flung myself into the role of investigative journalist. Starting with a friend of ours called Margaret who is the sanest person imaginable I decided to interview her two dogs and use them as examples of absolutely normal dogs with an absolutely normal owner.

'Hi Margaret,' I called, parking the car with some difficulty outside her cottage which had been built four hundred years before cars needed parking space. 'How are you?'

'Fraught,' said Margaret. 'Barney's been a devil today, haven't you, Barney?' Barney, her Jack Russell, wagged his tail when he saw I had brought Parsley and Ella with me and jumped up at the car. I opened the back and my two shot off into the woods yelping ecstatically when they saw rabbits bolting down holes. Margaret collared Barney and tied him to a long rope. 'Sorry about this, Barney,' she said, 'but I'm too tired to go chasing after you again.'

'What's he done?'

Over a cup of tea Margaret told me how Barney had committed the second most serious offence in a country dog's rulebook. He had gone absent without leave. Although he would never chase sheep the local farmers weren't to know that and if they saw a loose dog in a sheep field they were within their legal rights to shoot on sight. 'But I thought he was such a home-loving dog,' I said.

'He is,' said Margaret, 'but he met Geoffrey.' Geoffrey was Barney's friend. A spaniel from a nearby farm he was a Bad Influence on Barney and vice versa. Separately they were as good as gold but together they were anarchists, blind and deaf to their owners' whistles, hell bent on rabbitting, staying out late and generally behaving like youths who couldn't hold their beer.

This wouldn't do at all. I wanted normal dogs to start my research not hooligans. 'Would you say Barney was normal except when he's with Geoffrey?' I said, thinking I would be like other researchers and cheat. Margaret looked at Barney doubtfully. 'Well, er, have you seen the way he eats his dinner?' she said. I shook my head so she prepared Barney's meat and biscuits then fetched him in to the kitchen. Barney backed away from his dish. 'He's not hungry,' I said.

'Yes he is but he never eats if he thinks he's being watched.' Sure enough as soon as we stopped looking at him Barney ate his dinner.

That was the end of my research. Margaret is an old and valued friend, generous to the point of altruism and good without being goody goody. If she, of all people was the owner of an anarchic paranoid dog did it mean that she was a repressed something or other? If so I didn't want to know.

The other dog, Wanda, didn't really count as Margaret's as she had been a working guide dog for a blind woman and had only recently retired. Wanda must have regarded life with Margaret and Barney as a continuous lovely dream after all her years in harness. The cottage, sitting in a woodland clearing like a Beatrix Potter illustration, is surrounded by rabbit warrens and each evening hundreds of rabbits hop out of their burrows to graze. Wanda would sit and watch them, not quite believing the evidence of her highly trained eyes. Were they toys or dinners? Did one chase them or what? She was able to resolve her problem without loss of dignity when she found she was too old and stiff to have to make life or death decisions.

Our poor Ella, another pacifist like Wanda, had the opposite experience when she accidentally caught a rabbit one day. It was a very small buck and when I eventually arrived at the scene he was screaming blue murder. There was Ella looking guilty and elated at the same time with the baby rabbit held captive beneath her front paws. She had licked him from head to toe so he was quite soggy as well as being very very cross. I picked him up and dried him as best I could on my handkerchief. He kicked and struggled and swore revenge on all collies, a real little toughie. Ella was appalled at the racket he was making then, to her great relief, I posted the noisy infant down a rabbit hole. There was immediate silence. I could picture him down there, telling the tale to all his brothers and sisters: 'So I got this bloody great dog by the throat and I said to him I said . . .' Ella has been cautious since then. She still chases rabbits but if things look like getting serious she deliberately slows down. I have been cautious too, not asking Viv what it all symbolises.

Animals' names tell you quite a lot about their owners. It's not foolproof because some pets are secondhand and arrive complete with name, but broadly speaking dogs and cats with aristocratic human names are treated on equal terms in the family. They're not allowed total freedom, otherwise they would never go to the vet or have a bath, but within reason their opinions are respected and they have a say over things like outings, food, sleeping arrangements and holiday homes. A dog called Rover would *never* be offered a choice of boarding kennels at holiday time but would be sent to the nearest and cheapest. But a Harold or a Caroline would either be sent to a doggy equivalent of the Savoy or more likely be looked after by a house-sitter while the family went on holiday.

I'm always slightly apprehensive if dogs are called Thor, Mars, Satan or Nero. They usually have rather peculiar owners, fat little men who see themselves as whip-cracking lords and masters. (Fat little men without hang-ups call their dogs Cuddles or Spotty and are my most favourite customers.) Then there's the jokey brigade, with dogs called Dogma and cats with 'cat' in the name like Magnificat or Catullus. There are big dogs called Tiny and small dogs called Maxi. Biblical names are on the increase – I know two dogs, two humans and a horse all called Esther – as are names of towns – Worcester, Gloucester, Warwick. The alternative dogs of Totnes are called Gaia, I-Ching and Zen; herbal names like our own Parsley being quite popular too.

I once went to clip a couple of dogs called Daedalus and Icarus. It was somewhat puzzling to discover that both animals were bitches and that Icarus was the mother of Daedalus. When I asked why, the owners, a young couple with pots of money and not much in the way of manners, said it was a joke and

57

that I wouldn't understand. As the dogs (Schnauzers) looked like being good long-term customers I adopted a suitably dim-witted expression and got on with my work.

After about an hour the girl, who had been hovering in case I made off with the spoons, put the kettle on and made a pot of Earl Grey. She put it on a tray with two eggshell thin cups and saucers for herself and her husband. Then she opened a cupboard and got out a thick mug for me. Sod that, I thought. I hate tea in earthenware mugs, much too similar to flower pots, and as I had been very good about the dogs' gender I thought it was time for a peasants' revolt. 'I'd prefer a cup and saucer, if you wouldn't mind,' I said. 'It seems a pity to lose the flavour of good tea, doesn't it?' Fifteen love.

The girl who seemed hell bent on cramming me into her mental pigeonhole labelled 'lower orders' said she was intending to give me Typhoo. I made that fifteen all. 'Earl Grey is OK by me,' I said.

'*With* milk and sugar I suppose?' Thirty fifteen. She shouldn't have resorted to sarcasm.

'You'll ruin your palate if you mess up delicate teas with milk and sugar.' Forty fifteen.

We never finished the game nor was I ever booked for Icarus and Daedalus again.

In between dog clipping and green lane-ing we brought the glasshouses into use. The plan was to start the season with win-ter-flowering pansies and primulas then, as these cleared, to use the space for geraniums, fuchsias and begonias. But plants have a kind of Parkinson's Law of their own, they expand to fill the space available and then they expand again. It's a curious thing but no matter how much space a grower has it's never enough. Brian and I behaved like overcrowded rats, bickering and jostling in the greenhouses to ensure that our particular plants had their fair share of room. It was never a deliberate decision, this 'his' and 'her' business, it just came about. There was no dissension at first, we both love pansies and primulas and as we had only produced a few thousand there was plenty of room. But when these were gone and the summer-flowering cuttings were ready to take their place it was a different story.

The fuchsias arrived first, only a thousand and were quickly potted on into 4″ pots and lined up neatly in rows with a 12″ gap between the rows. Brian nipped off the growing tip of each one and put them in his propagator to root. Next came the geraniums, five hundred rooted cuttings of a very special strain called Fischers and a few hundred common ones. These too were potted on and placed in rows with a 12″ gap between the rows. By the time the non-stop begonia plantlets had been delivered the fuchsia cuttings in the propagator had taken root and needed potting on. You don't need to be good at sums to understand the mathematics of fuchsias. It's one equals another one.

Any gardening book will tell you how easy it is to strike a new fuchsia from the growing tip of its parent but they don't tell you how hard it is to break the habit. Even as I was laying out the begonias I was keeping a wary eye on Brian as he nipped out the growing tips of the second generation fuchsias. I began to wonder if there was life after greenhouse. 'Brian,' I said tactfully, 'are you going to keep *all* those cuttings?' He looked at the third thousand lying innocently in one seed tray (that's all the space they need as toddlers, the deceptive little horrors) and said it seemed a waste to throw them away. 'I'll find room for them, don't worry. You can move your begonias closer together.'

My begonias? Since when? I said: 'Oh I can, can I? How about you moving *your* geraniums closer together?'

You'd have thought I was expecting him to move his eyes closer together. 'My Fischers? You seriously want me to crowd Fischers?' These hallowed plants, according to the sales catalogue, were the Rolls Royces of geraniums, weather and disease resistant, prolific in habit and with non-fading flower colours. (For the record we have found all these claims to be accurate.) They were also twice the price of their common cousins.

'If they're so wonderful,' I said, 'they won't mind a bit of stress. It says in the catalogue how tolerant they are.'

Their tolerance apparently didn't extend to sharing a bed, and as I remained adamant over my begonias it was the fuchsias which had to suffer. Looking back on that season I think we were rather horrible to the fuchsias. There were certain varieties that neither of us liked very much, Cloverdale Pearl and Preston Guild in particular. We found them wishy washy insignificant specimens and it was these and some others like them that got crammed into the darkest recesses of the greenhouse. Call it racism or natural selection but these underprivileged plants failed to thrive. Some grew thin and leggy and some developed a rash. It was a vicious circle, the more unattractive the plants the more we felt justified in not liking them to start with and moving them even further into earwiggy corners.

The greenhouses reached saturation point. Gone were the 12″ gaps between the rows, you couldn't have put a matchstick between them, and watering became a test of co-ordination skills. Carefully balancing on the raised bed retaining walls you had to aim the hose jet into each flowerpot in turn as you picked your way along the ledges. The trick was to control the force of the jet (Brian used an expensive brass nozzle, I used my thumb) so that it was strong enough to reach the pots at the back but not so fierce as to send all the pots tumbling like dominoes. The begonia plantlets, by virtue of their extreme youth, were watered from the bottom. They stood in grit beds and so successful was this early treatment – wet feet dry heads – that I continued it into their adulthood and we achieved a mild fame for their quality.

We had just got the overcrowding problem nicely under control (by agreeing not to strike any more cuttings) when suddenly we had a fresh population explosion on our hands.

My sixteen cowslip plants which I had raised from a bought packet of seed, bloomed beautifully, died down and set seed. I had had a very poor germination from the original seed even though I followed the packet instructions to the letter and this time, determined to do better, I got out all our gardening books and took notes. Hardly any of the experts agreed on cowslip propagation and even those that did seemed to me to have got

60

it wrong. What they recommended was planting the seed in a light loam in trays and placing the trays in a warm but shady position. Well that's exactly what I had done before and only sixteen plants had appeared. But in a tattered old book without any covers I found an opposing view. This writer said cowslips needed light and *cold* to trigger germination. I went straight out with a pair of scissors and collected the seed heads from my sixteen plants. These I winnowed into a pudding basin and as some of them were still green I spread them out on a windowsill to ripen. Being rather impatient I only allowed them half an hour – they probably needed a couple of weeks – before dividing them into four tiny heaps. Each heap was then sprinkled on to a separate seed tray containing nothing but damp silver sand and left *uncovered*. The tattered book writer had definitely said light and cold and my seeds were going to have the lightest coldest induction possible. I slid each seed tray into a thick polythene bag to stop evaporation and put the trays at the bottom of a north facing wall which never received direct sunlight. Not that the position was particularly important as it was one of those summers when nobody got much direct sunlight.

A couple of weeks later Brian, who gets up at dawn every day to make sure everything in the garden is where it was the night before, came in for breakfast and reported that we had lift off in the cowslip trays. Our boiled eggs were like bullets by the time I had finished admiring my new babies, *all five thousand of them.*

'I can't believe it,' I kept saying. 'How can sixteen plants produce five thousand?'

'It's only three hundred and something a plant,' said Brian, but even he had to admit the germination rate was extraordinary. Was it because the seed had been so fresh?

Experienced gardeners and/or devotees of detective novels will have guessed by now that there was something fishy about a hundred per cent germination. (See clue on page 8.) We didn't, even though we are both these things. All we worried about was where the hell could we house the new arrivals. 'How about the spare bedroom?' I suggested.

'They're not *that* hardy,' said Brian. 'Look, would you mind if we threw away about half? I could probably make enough cold frames for two or three thousand but even that would be pushing it with so little space.'

'Throw away cowslips? We'd never be able to show our faces in Totnes again. Friends of the Earth would put out a contract on us, Preservation of Rural England would chuck petrol bombs through the letter box, you'd have your subscription to the Henry Doubleday . . .'

'All right, all right, we'll keep them. But we can't prick out all of them – they don't bloom for a year, you know.'

I'd forgotten that. It meant pricking them out, potting them on, then keeping them housed, fed and watered until they reached point of sale in eleven months' time. There was no way we could spare the time and space. Some would have to go.

Friends were presented with a tablespoonful of cowslip seedlings whether they wanted them or not. A tablespoon doesn't sound very many but in fact once they were untangled there were fifty to a hundred in each clump. We ran out of friends long before we ran out of seedlings. Brian and the green laners planted some in selected green lanes which is going to look rather odd when the survey records are published. Will anyone wonder why cowslips seem to be confined to a small radius round Totnes?

Next I had the romantic notion of combining the dogs' evening walks with cowslip planting sprees. The dogs would romp in the fields while I arranged my cowslips prettily round the edges. Ha ha. For a start I couldn't reach the edges without hacking a path through nettles and brambles, and on the one or two occasions I did do some planting Parsley suspected me of burying bones and did some un-planting of her own. Conservationists were another hazard. You wouldn't believe how hard it is to do a good deed in some pockets of rural Devon. The conservationists have nearly always beaten you to it and planted up 'your' pasture with so many rare orchids, ragged robin, etc. that you have to avoid treading on their treasures while you hunt out a suitable site for your own.

All the while we were scattering cowslips around the country-side there were *still* seeds germinating in the trays so it was a case of running up a moving escalator. We estimated in the end that the sixteen parent plants had been responsible for six thousand seedlings. We kept back three thousand to grow on and still scratched our heads over what to do with the surplus.

But happily some friends of ours Raymond and Valerie, professional nurserymen, offered to take a whole trayful. They were in the process of phasing out their cut-flower business in favour of retail plant selling and were always on the lookout for supplies of unusual plants. 'Good quality,' said Raymond, running an experienced eye over the seedlings. 'It'll be nice to have something a bit different to offer our customers next year.'

Just *how* different was the cowslips' own secret, not to be revealed until the following spring.

Chapter Seven

BRIAN ISN'T ALWAYS very imaginative about choosing birthday or Christmas presents but when my birthday came round he made up for previous lapses. He bought me eight hundred worms.

This seems a peculiar number but the reason was simple. Worm starter kits come by post and as it would be unkind to send live adult worms through the post they send capsules (worm eggs) instead, each capable of hatching out four wormlets. My kit comprised two hundred capsules, starter box, bedding and instructions.

The worm equivalent of Heinz baby food is leaf mould so into the nursery went bedding, then capsules then a topping of leaf mould. Later they would eat horse manure and kitchen waste, a diet guaranteed to keep them so deliriously happy that they would stay within bounds – A Happy Worm Will Not Leave Home – and breed. The capsules needed a hatching temperature of around 60°F. I started them off in the greenhouse but it was too hot by day and too cold at night so I brought them indoors, the *only* time in our entire married life that Brian and I have not come to blows over livestock in the kitchen.

A fortnight or so later they began to hatch, tiny pink threads which soon turned brownish red and burrowed deep into the leaf mould. Although worms are surface feeders they will avoid light and I was unable to keep any hatching records as they tended to vanish whenever I tried to count them. Matthew popped in when they were ten weeks old and we tipped the entire nursery on to some newspaper for him to give a professional opinion. The hatching had not been at all even (probably my fault for continually uncovering them and probing around to see what they were up to) and while one or two were showing signs of sexual maturity there were still quite a few which hadn't even left their capsules. Matthew said I should ignore the non-starters and transfer the whole nursery to a permanent place of work.

Accordingly I dug a pit in a dark corner of one of the greenhouses which was too dark even for an unloved fuchsia. I put a thin layer of peat at the bottom followed by the young worms and half a barrow of horse manure. A mildly dotty friend of mine claims to be able to increase her worms' appetites by heating their food but I drew the line at warmed up dung. Taking a leaf out of Darwin's book I did experiment with different kinds of food. Darwin's worms showed a marked preference for beetroot and onion. So did mine. In one of my early trials I placed apples, peeled bananas, potatoes, carrots, turnips, beetroot and onion round the edges of the wormery. The worms ate all the beetroot and onion first, then the rest in no particular order. I wanted to see if it was the taste or the consistency that attracted them so next time I left the beetroot and onion in lumps but mashed up the other vegetables. Again they took the beetroot and onion first so I concluded that worms have a definite sense of taste.

In their seasons I tried salads and exotic fruits but, conservative to a worm, my colony *still* preferred beetroot to mango or onion to strawberry. There was one treat which was the exception to their rule and this was fuchsia seed heads. Once these have ripened and turned black they're delicious (and safe) to eat – sweet and slightly nutty.

The experimental foods were offered in addition to their staple diet of horse manure. I didn't want to encourage faddy eaters but I did want to know what made them such efficient converters. (One pound of worms eats one pound of food and excretes one pound of casts a day.) They started breeding and I had to dig another pit. Worms are hermaphrodites, when boy meets girl they both get pregnant which is a nice companionable arrangement when you think about it. Their mating patterns were companionable too. It's not easy to do a Kinsey report on worms but as far as I could tell they did it in groups, coiling around several friends at once, like Totnes teenagers.

When they weren't doing that they were eating beetroot and I was reasonably sure that they were having a nice time.

American worms on the other hand have not been having a nice time lately. Some mad scientists tried feeding them on mono-diets ranging from lettuce to plums. The idea was to produce the 'Wormburger', that is to say worm meat with a good flavour but it came unstuck when the scientists met with consumer resistance. Wormburgers, no matter how flavoursome did not appeal to the American public. Too gritty, said the testers and the researchers had to go back to the drawing board. They found that the worms were retaining minute particles of grit in their colons which, no matter how thoroughly the 'meat' was washed, remained detectable. Clever American worms. They seem to have cracked the secret of being inedible.

When the time came to start selling our summer-flowering plants one of our outlets was through car boot sales. At the first one we ever went to I was rummaging through a secondhand bookstall when I found an old *Lilliput* with, of all things, a worm poem in it. I rushed back to our stall where poor Brian was trying to get the customers into some sort of queue (plant stalls are the second most popular after cakes) and to his acute embarrassment read him the poem. It was in a collection by John Pudney entitled Low Life.

> Admire the worm who canalises life,
> Who seeks no territory, influence or pal,
> Attention from an undertaker or a wife,
> All life goes through his alimentary canal.

'It's a bloody awful poem,' Brian snarled. 'Now will you stop *buying* and come and help me *sell*.'

'Sorry,' I said and I was. But car boot sales were a whole new world to me and I had no will power. I put my shopping bag full of treasure trove into the car to be gloated over later at home (car boot sales reveal far more of the dark side of oneself than cats) and joined Brian behind the stall.

Business was brisk not to say violent. Women trained in the martial arts at jumble sales make formidable car booters. Brian, who had never attended a jumble sale, watched with anthropological interest as two members of the gentler sex slogged it out using their highly tuned elbows. 'Ladies,' he said tentatively, 'I've got plenty more geraniums. Look, here are some more of the same sort . . .'

I giggled. 'You don't know the rules. They both want that particular one.'

'Why?'

'Because they think they saw it first. They'll sort themselves out in a minute; you don't need to interfere.'

Baffled, Brian transferred another six geraniums of the same variety from the car to the stall. They were called Schöne Helena (one of the Fischers) and looking at them objectively we had to admit they were worth fighting for. Schöne Helena is described in the catalogue as large flowered, salmon pink, semi-double with attractive white edging to the petals and light-zoned leaves.They never really go overboard in catalogues. They could have said that Schöne Helena is a breeder's masterpiece, exquisitely beautiful, grows as strong as a tree and produces at least twelve flower branches at any one time if it's grown properly.

The two ladies settled their disagreement and asked us to put their purchases on one side to be collected later. Some other customers wanted theirs minded too and soon we had a fine old muddle of geraniums, fuchsias and begonias on the grass round the car. 'Do you know whose is what?' I said, when the first flurry had died down and people were bargain hunting elsewhere.

'I think so,' Brian said. 'But they'll remember what they bought, won't they?'

When the customers did return to collect their plants some remembered exactly what they had chosen but others only said they did. As everyone had paid beforehand we left them to bicker among themselves. There was no actual bloodshed but we made a note to bring a felt tip pen next time so that we could write their names on the pots.

Brian went off to look round the other stalls while I minded

67

the shop. It was good fun being part of the hurly-burly, part camp part market and listening to the bartering going on. This was in the early days of car boot sales when everyone was there to enjoy themselves and maybe make a few pounds from their attic junk and homemade jam. (In later sales dealers began poking their unwelcome noses into 'our' scene and all but ruined the wonderfully matey atmosphere.)

'If you want to go round with your hubby I'll keep an eye on your stall.' This was from a woman on one side of us who appeared to have everything including the kitchen sink on her stall.

'Go round with him?' I said in horror. 'Do you go shopping with your husband?'

She laughed. 'I would if I was married to yours. You haven't been watching but so far he's bought a lawnmower and some other bits of machinery and a big box of something.' It was so utterly out of character for Brian to scrum down round a junk stall I wondered what had got into him. It didn't matter. A boot sale is only an up-market jumble sale and nobody bankrupts themselves when the prices seldom go above pence. I decided not to worry and got on with serving a pair of grandmotherly women. They stood around chatting afterwards. The first one said to her friend 'How's Lynn?' and then asked after other members of the family finishing with 'and your sister's boy? The one who went to Australia – did he get a job?'

The other one said: 'Yes, right on the Bonsai Beach. Of course they had to amputate, I dare say you heard?'

'Mm,' said the first. 'Poor lamb. Mind you it could have been worse. I always think it's a blessing we're born with so many to start with . . .' They strolled out of earshot and I nearly abandoned the stall to follow them. Born with so many *what* for heaven's sake? And what sort of job could the carved up nephew do on the Bonsai Beach?

Brian came back. Before I could say why do we need a fourth grass cutter we had a second wave of customers. 'This looks unusual,' said someone picking up one of our least praiseworthy fuchsias. Smarmily pretending to like it Brian said,

'It's called Preston Guild,' and I took the cue and added, 'Blue and white. You don't see many blue fuchsias, do you?' We had a sneaking suspicion that the blueness was probably due to cardiac arrest brought on by being stuck away in the damp recesses of the greenhouse for so long.

'I'll take two, please.' Predictably, for bargain hunters invariably buy the same as the person in front of them, people began to snap up the Preston Guilds. (Later in the year these same fuchsias planted out properly in their new owners' gardens grew vigorous and sturdy which I think proves what TLC can do.) Our stall was emptying and the margarine-carton cash box nice and heavy. Brian lightened it considerably by scooping out a handful of coins. 'Just popping over to pay for my, er, my things,' he muttered and went off again. I stepped over the grass cutter and opened his mysterious cardboad box. Inside was a power-driven hedge cutter which, if it worked, would be a welcome relief from person-powered shears or horse-powered teeth. He also bought a water pump (we have no pond) and a complete set of Waverley novels for 10p. I groaned and our stall neighbour laughed and said she *had* warned me. Brian had caught boot-sale fever, the disease which in its later more serious stage compels its victims to bid beyond their means at auction sales.

Luckily the bookstall man understood the symptoms and took back the Waverley novels. 'Did he only write for the jumble trade?' he asked, meaning Walter Scott.

'Why don't you put them out for the dustmen?' I suggested.

'They won't take them. Too heavy, and I don't like to put them out one at a time. Funny about books, no matter how awful they are you don't like to split up a set. Know what I mean?'

We dismantled our stall, called goodbye to our new stallholder acquaintances and went home well pleased with our selling and buying. Among my treasures was a photograph frame. When I wiped the glass I found it contained a black and white snapshot of a small and rather appealing mongrel. 'Benjy 1927' it said on the back. Benjy must have been very special. Not only had he had a photograph frame all to himself but the picture had

69

been tinted in the fashion of the day. I had intended putting a photograph of one of the children in the frame but I changed my mind and laid one of Ella on top of Benjy. It would be nice to think that sometime in the next century when our household junk ends up at a spaceship boot sale someone will find Ella and Benjy and wonder a bit about them.

When we told Marcus about our new boot sale craze and how you can get practically anything for a song he wrote back: 'I've met a widow with ten children in Burma, desperately poor. Can you send some clothes?' There were no helpful details of sizes or sexes of the children and rather than wait for his next letter we thought we had better send something quickly.

At the next two sales we bought over forty items from cotton dresses to shorts and pullovers. Mostly it was new stuff or nearly new and looked very gay and colourful piled up in the spare room. I folded everything as tightly as possible and Brian, who is a champion packer, packed it all into a huge brown paper sack. We had intended sending it by airmail to save time but that would have cost sixty pounds which seemed an awful lot of money. So we sent it by surface mail for twenty pounds and wrote to Marcus suggesting that in future it might be better to send money instead.

By this time Marcus had left Burma – they only let tourists stay a fortnight – and gone on to Delhi. He wrote saying don't send money to the widow as she had now taken to drink. (Who wouldn't?) 'Carry on sending her clothes,' he said, 'I'll pay the postage.'

We would have been pleased to continue clothing the family but sadly our first and only parcel never arrived. Marcus had given the address of a convent that was helping the widow and I wrote separately to the Mother Superior and to the widow herself but we had no replies at all. The post to and from these countries is notoriously bad – Marcus lost fifty pounds of honey bound for London – but what sort of person would steal a parcel of children's clothes?

70

On a happier note Marcus told us the story of how he was attacked by bandits. Obviously this wasn't a happier note for him but his description tickled us. In broad daylight on the streets of Delhi he had been beaten up and robbed. 'I couldn't defend myself,' he said, 'as these were lady bandits.'

These 'ladies', a grim trio from the sound of it, had probably known that Englishmen don't fight women and had grabbed poor unsuspecting Marcus from behind and proceeded to duff him up. When he came round he found himself with no rucksack, money belt or passport so he went straight to the nearest police station.

'What followed was worse than being robbed,' he wrote. 'The cops were dreadfully apologetic and some of them stayed to see to me and some went rushing out to apprehend (their word) the women who were well known for ambushing foreigners. They caught them and dragged them inside the police station. All my stuff was OK, they hadn't had time to get rid of it, so I told the head copper I didn't want to make a thing of it but he wouldn't listen. He ordered his sidekicks to give them a beating. I think he thought he was being polite and proving to me that they know how to look after tourists. Anyway all the women got a walloping, they made an awful noise about it and that made me feel awful too, as if it was my fault. Then they let them go. I suppose it saves a lot of paperwork, doling out punishment on the spot but I can't say I'm keen.'

Some of the newspaper cuttings he sends home from time to time are unintentionally funny too. There was one headline – it was about another crime altogether – which said COPS NAB MISCREANT IN POSH DISTRICT. Many Indian reporters seem to have been educated on a mixture of Galsworthy and the *Beano*. The word 'posh' is commonly used in India but Marcus said he had never seen 'nab' in a newspaper before. Another cutting was about the escape from a lunatic asylum of all the inmates. The place was short staffed and the patients (who are still called lunatics in India), fed up with the filthy conditions inside, broke out and scattered into the surrounding countryside. The article concluded with: 'The lunatics will be easily identifiable by their total absence of attire.' But the funniest one was a printing error. A nuclear weapons expert answering a question about safety had replied: 'The warhead is programmed not to explode before launch,' but the printers had put 'before lunch'. What a fitting end it would be for this planet to go out on a printer's error.

Chapter Eight

FROM TIME TO TIME, when it becomes obvious that our current car won't be well enough to pass its next MOT, we buy another one before the old one dies. One of these two-car periods fell during the car boot sale season which couldn't have been more convenient. Brian would go to work in one and when he came home, if it was a boot sale day, I would have the other one loaded up ready to go out. As it took at least an hour to load up properly this saved us valuable selling time and sometimes meant that we got a good pitch and not the boggy corners that were the fate of latecomers.

I looked forward to the evening expeditions. After the heat of the day, much of which was spent sweltering inside the glasshouses it was lovely to get out. The venues varied and after some trial and error we found a pattern that suited. Every other Wednesday we went to a cricket club grounds, Tuesdays were school playing field days, one Monday a month there was a field next to a village pub, and so on. We avoided concrete whenever possible as it was too hot in the early part of the evening and we also avoided Totnes in case our 'pot plants' notice was misunderstood.

Brian quite liked the evening outings too, not as much as I did because he had already put in a day's work and was tired. (The work people do at home is never considered as work.) Also he would have preferred a home-cooked supper but as I pointed out – repeatedly – there wasn't time for me to prepare a meal after an evening on the stall. There was plenty of time actually but I'll grasp at the flimsiest of straws to avoid cooking. The meals we did have were far nicer than mine in any case. One of our fellow stallholders sold big juicy Cornish pasties still warm from the oven and if we could control ourselves long enough to get them home intact I would reheat them and serve them with our own freshly picked tomatoes and cucumber. If the Cornish pasty lady didn't come we would have fish and chips or a Chinese take-away. I really loved the evening boot sales.

So as not to miss any opportunities we started taking an evening paper which gave dates of forthcoming local events including boot sales and through these we were able to book a stall at one or two village fêtes at weekends. Fêtes were much more leisurely affairs than boot sales. There was time to set up the stall properly without getting squashed in the rush of customers, time too for a wander round and maybe have a few goes at skittles or coconut shying. Brian has an ambivalent attitude to fêtes. He claims he was traumatised at a fête as a young man and has never forgotten it.

He wasn't really traumatised at all, he was just soaking wet but it's true that he hasn't forgotten. He and I had met at a party the previous evening. I've always detested parties and had only gone to keep a girlfriend company. The din was awful and as my friend seemed to be having a good time I thought it would be all right to slip away quietly and go home. As I was leaving Brian arrived. Someone introduced us and I said hello and goodbye and headed for the street. Brian said, 'Why are you going, are you ill?'

'It's late,' I said.

He said in astonishment, 'It's *ten o'clock*, for God's sake!' I said ten o'clock was a funny time to arrive at a party and that I was going to bed. He followed me outside and waited while I found my car keys. There was a gleam in his eye which I mistook for lust; hindsight proved it was not my body he was after but the fifteen-seater minibus I happened to be driving at the time. (I don't mean he wasn't after both, just that to a busy florist a girl is only a girl whereas a good big bus is a rarity.) He asked for my phone number. I said, 'I'll be at the Highgate fête tomorrow afternoon.' I didn't add that I would have a gang of small children with me. People who start their social life halfway through the night wouldn't like children.

The bus I was driving belonged to a school for handicapped

children that employed me to ferry them about. Brian was under the impression that I owned it but as I was under the impression that he was the writer Brian Aldiss honours were even.

It was sunny on the morning of the Highgate fête but soon after lunch the sun went in and a steady grey drizzle took over. Paradoxically, Londoners are much tougher in bad weather than their country cousins, or perhaps they're not as sensible; at any rate the fête continued as planned and nobody took cover. To my great surprise Brian showed up. He was wearing a green and brown pure silk shirt which I instantly coveted. (If I'd known what a devil it was to iron I wouldn't have been so keen to get my hands on it.)

We strolled around getting colder and wetter by the minute. I asked him why he wrote science fiction and he asked me how many miles the bus did to the gallon and by the time the double disillusionment had set in we were soaked literally to the skin. There was a huge pile of grass cuttings fermenting at the edge of the field and we made for this and stood on it, grateful for the warmth it was giving off. Our feet sank deep into the heart of the pile; the grass juices oozed up our legs leaving green stains, and a gentle steam enveloped us. 'Well, that's better,' I said. Brian stared at the sky and said nothing as rain dripped from the leaves above and found its way into the top of his light blue jeans which were already ruined from the compost below. Eventually he came out of his stupor. 'I hope,' he said, 'I just hope I don't see anyone here that I know.'

A relationship founded in a compost heap can't help but get better. We were married not long afterwards and as our mothers said at the time it served us both right.

Things seemed to have come full circle when fête day after fête day fell in bad weather. Stallholders selling knitwear and other dry goods would look enviously at our plant stall as they fought to lay sheets of polythene over their tables in the cold wind. Although we didn't have to protect our stuff we still had to try and sell it, and not many people wanted dripping wet plants messing up their cars.

At one fête there was a family dog show which my mother, in a fit of wanting to show some support, entered with Inky and Melly. It was raining so hard that only two other dog owners were brave enough to enter. (The dogs had no say in the matter.) The four dogs paraded – trawled would be a better description – round the ring while the desperate judge kept wiping his clipboard to stop the ink running. There were several classes: Best Veteran, Dog Most Like Its Owner, Dog with Waggiest Tail and Dog the Judge Would Most Like to Take Home. Nobody in their right mind would want to take a soggy dog home but the judge had to get rid of the prizes somehow and Inky and Melly swept the board.

I could understand Melly winning the Most Like to Take Home because she was the smallest of the four, but when the judge awarded the red rosette to Inky for having the Waggiest Tail I felt honour bound to say something. 'She hasn't got a tail,' I said.

'Hasn't she? Oh shit,' said the judge. 'Well never mind. Let's say she's the least miserable dog in the ring.' And off he ran to the tea tent.

'It could only happen to an alternative dog,' said Anne smugly.

Later on the weather cleared and the organisers set up a different doggy event – handicap races. This was the big time stuff, with tote betting on each race. The dogs wore a number tied round their chests and paraded in the collecting ring like race-horses. If there was a particularly fast-looking dog the betting would reach the dizzy heights of 3p or even 5p. The handicapping procedure was a matter of summing up the chances of, say, a small fat dachshund against an Afghan and giving the smaller dog thirty or so yards' start.

There was much dispute over the fairness of the handicaps, particularly if the handicapper was related to the racedog owner, and blatant nobbling in the form of chocolate trails which stopped short of the winning post. Prizes were given to the first three dogs in each heat and there was a special prize for the dog that showed the most 'character'. (This was won by a labrador who waited for the starter to say go then turned his back on the race and went home.)

After all the heats had been run the winners lined up for the final. Ten dogs ranging from the sublime to the ridiculous took up their positions. The handicapper went round and moved the little ones forward while the bookie called the changing odds and took bets. Everyone's money was on a whippet which had won its qualifying heat by several lengths.

'Go,' said the starter. The dogs bounded forwards encouraged by their owners who were standing at the winning post a hundred yards away. A Yorkshire terrier and a Jack Russell started fighting and the rest of the field had to jump over or round the bundle of flying fur as they pressed on. The odds on favourite gained ground steadily, overtaking spaniels, labradors and alsatians. Someone stopped for a pee and his owner called out 'You're not *that* handicapped.' Other owners shouted 'walkies' which seemed a bit tame in the circumstances and others urged their pets to do things which would be frowned upon at Newmarket or Epsom. Still the whippet came on and just when it looked as though nobody could overtake it a black and white collie made a final heroic effort and flung itself over the line first. There was a groan from the crowd. Everybody, including the collie's owner, had bet on the whippet. The winning-post judge, an old hand at village politics, called out to the bookie: 'Whippet first, Bob; collie second, spannul third.' The punters collected their winnings and all the humans were satisfied. The collie probably went home and wrote to his M.P.

Being a judge at an English village show calls for qualities not unlike those of a trained professional soldier: courage under fire, quick thinking and an ability to melt away in the bushes when things get dangerous. If a judge can cultivate a reputation for mild eccentricity beforehand it helps because by the end of the proceedings, when he or she has become clinically unhinged, not too many people will notice.

In most shows there are classes for fruit, flowers, vegetables, 'produce' (chutney to sponge cakes), flower arrangements, art

– this can mean anything – and lots more. 'It's only a small friendly affair.' This is the standard opening gambit for organisers when they are reduced to doing a house to house search for someone (anyone) daft enough to agree to judge a class. The OED defines friendly as 'on amicable terms'. Village show organisers extend this definition to include anybody who hasn't actually shot dead the person who comes between him and his chances of a prizewinning leek. If the adult classes are hard to judge, the children's section is impossible.

A friend's daughter foolishly let herself be persuaded to judge 'Mixed Pets' once. The children filed in, each carrying a cardboard box or restraining the family dog on a lead, and arranged themselves on straw bales in a semi-circle. With mounting unease the judge started going round. She patted dogs, stroked rabbits and guinea pigs, avoided rats and hoped nobody had brought a python. One little girl didn't appear to have a pet then at the last minute produced a matchbox containing a hairy caterpillar. All the children were expected to answer questions about their pets' welfare and the little caterpillar girl passed her viva with ease. She knew what it ate, where its natural habitat was and moreover what it was going to turn into. Thanks to its owner's grasp of entomology the hairy caterpillar automatically became a contender for the red rosette, on equal terms with pedigree dogs and the rest. The judge moved on, only too horribly aware that if she awarded first prize to a caterpillar the other children's mothers were going to be baying for her blood. The next child's pet was a cockatoo. 'Does he talk?' asked the judge, leaning forward to examine the bird. The small owner nodded. 'Words,' she said. 'He says lots of words.' The judge said lots of words too, but under her breath, when she tried to move away and found her finger held fast by the cockatoo's beak.

It would have been nice to hear how that particular class ended but our friend's daughter says her recollection of events after she had been bitten by the parrot is nil. It could be that she *did* put the caterpillar among the prizewinners and the amnesia was brought on by having her head kicked in by a disappointed mother. Queensberry rules don't apply to village fêtes.

In the classified ads column of a local paper someone was offering a 'ciné to video' service, something quite new a few years back. We phoned for details and learned that providing one's old ciné films are not too dilapidated they can be trans ferred on to video film relatively cheaply. We have never had any projection equipment but we did still have several 8mm ciné films of the children when they were small. We got them out, unrolled them and held them up to the light. They were in amazingly good shape considering their age – very few breaks and plenty of colour left in the emulsion, so we decided to have them processed.

The man who did the work made sure, by tactful and euphemistic questioning, that our films weren't pornographic then, when he had made the new film, he phoned up and asked if we would like a musical sound-track at no extra cost. As he said, a one and a half hour silent film can be a bit taxing. Without giving it much thought Brian said OK to music and rang off.

'What sort of music?' I asked.

'He didn't say.'

'But Brian it might be awful. Didn't he give a clue about what sort?'

'He said music appropriate to the age of the film.'

We didn't like to phone back as the music was coming free but decided if it was Sandy McPherson or Wagner we would simply turn the sound off. (Not that we have any sound to turn off, we don't have a video ourselves but our friends Kevin and Denise had recently bought one.)

A few days later we went to collect the film and were shown into a viewing room. 'I'll just run it through quickly for you – show you a few scenes to make sure you're satisfied with the quality,' the man said. I don't want a penny from you unless you're satisfied with the work.' Here was someone who had evidently never been connected with the building trade. He switched on and a group of total strangers appeared on the screen and started to walk towards the camera laughing and waving then there was a smooth cut to a swan gliding up the Thames. 'Nice cutting,' I said politely. Who on earth were these people? 'Thank you,' said the man, rather puzzled that we hadn't started saying, 'Oh look, there's Auntie Flo . . .' the way most people do when they see twenty-year-old home movies. Other strangers came and went (we still hadn't realised they were us), the swan was joined by three cygnets and there were several minutes of cinematic indulgences – close ups of baby birds, long shots of power boats churning up a lather of water and the inevitable sunset. Just as we were wondering how to tell the man he was showing us someone else's film our old dog Honey, magically transformed back to a six-week-old puppy came on the screen. 'Honey,' we chorused and leaned forward in our seats. 'Our dog,' I explained unnecessarily to the man. 'She died a year ago. She was nearly seventeen.' He didn't say anything but wound the film on quickly, probably afraid that we'd be asking for Kleenex if he left the puppy on too long.

That poor man. Every time I think of what happened next I get a fit of the giggles. He slowed the film and by an awful coincidence it was a shot of a friend's dog, an alsatian called Ricky who had had to be put to sleep following an accident. 'Look, Brian, that's Ricky,' I said. 'Pity he had to be put down, wasn't it?' Quickly the film was whizzed forward and *again* it stopped at a deceased friend, a human one this time, who had died of pneumonia in U.C.H. 'Do you remember Alf . . .?' Brian gave me a hard nudge in the ribs.

By some superhuman effort of willpower we suppressed our giggles, gulping and choking into our handkerchiefs as yet more dead beings were revitalised on the screen. The final toll not counting rabbits was seven: four animal and three human – Honey, Ricky, Alf, Katie, Boots, Fred, Taffy. Quite a cenotaph. Obviously in twenty years a proportion of one's circle is going to shuffle off but what was so uncanny was the way the film always managed to slow on the now dead. Brian whispered: 'He must be thinking we used the ciné camera as a lethal weapon.' That did it. Slumped down in our seats, moaning now with the stomach ache that comes from bottled up laughter, we must have looked as though we were in the throes of deep grief. Considerately the man switched off the film and put the lights on. 'Did you like the music?' he asked. 'I thought the Beatles would be just right seeing that the film was made in the sixties.' We assured him as best we could through our hiccups that we liked the sound-track (what sound-track?), paid, and escaped with the precious video. Brian drove a little way down the road then stopped the engine and at last we were able to let ourselves go. The car windows steamed up, goodness knows what passers-by imagined was going on, and the puzzled dogs scrambled over the backs of the seats and licked our faces.

We carried on home, Brian driving carefully in his weakened state, and phoned our still alive friends Kevin and Denise. Brian explained that we had a video film but no player and invited ourselves round to use theirs. 'You can't come until this evening,' Kevin said firmly. 'Denise is up to her ears in, er, in alterations.' Denise did antique lace repairs for a friend of hers who had an antique shop. Mostly it was old tablecloths and napkins that she repaired, nothing as far as we knew that came under the heading of 'alterations'. We thought no more about it until we arrived at their house at eight o'clock.

Kevin opened the door, a half empty glass in his hand, and we went into the sitting room where Denise was putting the finishing touches to six large white garments spread out over the back of an armchair. 'Victorian bloomers,' she said.

'For a museum?' asked Brian.

'No silly, for *wearing*. They're all the rage with youngsters – you must have seen girls going to parties in them?' Brian said he hadn't and I said how could you appear in public wearing something with a big split in the crutch? (Victorian bloomers were made open plan for going to the loo.) Denise said: 'I've been altering them,' and held up a finished pair. The split had been neatly sewn up and some of the voluminous sides taken in, the final effect being rather nautical except for the lace trimmings.

Kevin poured us a drink and seemed anxious to get off the subject of Victorian bloomers. 'How are Marcus and Sara?' he said.

'Fine,' we said. 'And how are Marie-France and Geraldine? Home from College yet?'

'No. They've both taken holiday jobs abroad, we shan't see them until term starts.'

'Just as well,' I said. 'If they saw these they'd pester you to buy them a pair.' Marie-France and Geraldine were at the forefront of teenage fashion, nothing was too short or too long or too weird to be included in their wardrobes. Great Grandmama's underwear would be right up their street.

'I wish one of them was here,' Denise said, indicating the bloomers, 'Kevin's been . . .'

'Have another drink,' interrupted Kevin.

'Kevin's been what?' said Brian curiously.

'. . . modelling for me. But I'd have preferred one of the girls.'

Flabbergasted, Brian stared at Kevin. '*Modelling* those knickers? With frilly ends and everything?'

'Lace trim,' said Denise automatically. For the second time that day we collapsed, picturing Kevin's hairy muscular legs in the daintily frilled bloomers. Kevin defended himself by describing the situation as an emergency. Denise's antique shop friends needed the bloomers for a customer and Denise, finding the alterations virtually impossible without a girl to try them on, had persuaded ('She *forced* me, Brian') Kevin to step into the breeches as it were. He had flatly refused to model the garments in the sitting room in case someone saw him through the window so the business had been done in their hallway with Kevin jumping out of his skin every time he thought he heard a caller at the front door.

'How on earth did you manage to pin the material in?' I asked. 'Kevin's the wrong shape for a girl.' Kevin said coldly he had never had any complaints in that department and could we please stop talking about bloomers and get on with the video film?

Chapter Nine

HALFWAY DOWN the main street in Totnes is a barber's shop sign which reads: HAIRDRESSING FOR ALTERNATIVE MEN. I have often toyed with the idea of changing the wording on my own card in the pet-shop window to the canine equivalent of the barber's sign but lack the nerve. There's a 'town and gown' division in Totnes and if I was to ally myself to gown the conformist dogs would probably withdraw their custom.

Geographically near but a million miles away in culture is Torbay. Ribbon developments of bungalows called Gwenbill and Bobjoy have eaten up the beautiful Devon redsoil. Older people who knew the region as children abandoned the sinking ship and moved to proper houses in proper villages and the newly retired with amalgamated names moved in. As a dog lady I go where the work is, from near stately homes to mobile homes, and since there's no law to stop Gwenbill and Bobjoy from keeping a dog I go to Bungoland too. But what a performance. Out come dustsheets and ghastly little hand-held gadgets which in Totnes would be regarded as sexual stimulants but which Gwenbill and Bobjoy have bought for *hoovering up toast crumbs*. (I'm not making this up.) As I clip the poor little non-iron dog one or other partner will stand at my elbow, triumphantly sucking up every stray wisp of fur before it gets a chance to spread the Black Death on the floor.

Sometimes, but thank God not very often, everyone in Bungoland wants their dog done on the same day. It's as though they wake up, see the sun shining and say to each other: 'Coo look, Gwenbill, what a lovely day! Let's wash the curtains and the dog and the car.' 'Good idea, Gwenbill. I'll phone the dog lady and you can make a start with that nice car vacuum I bought you for Christmas.' On one such day I visited Ruff,

Sandy and Misty from Treveen, Ivydave and Salmatt. The two Salmatts were not amused when I said if the Matt half had been called Adrian they could have called their house Salad.)

Reeling from the anaesthetising effect of shampoo, flea spray and air freshener and sighing for the ozone layer I drove to my last call of the day, someone I hadn't seen to before, at a house called Land Ahoy. Mrs Land Ahoy was a widow and totally, but totally round the bend. She opened the door and the first thing she said was: 'I don't like the look of you.' As she had a face like a weasel and hair dyed bright ginger I thought she was a fine one to talk. True to my judo training I held my fire and waited to see what the opponent would do next. She took a step backwards into her hall and beckoned me in but I'd got no further than the doormat when she started shouting. 'You don't have to wipe your feet, you won't find my savings under the mat.' Leaving the door open in case she had a six foot son as barmy as herself I went further into the hall. This set her off again: 'Don't you dare touch the wallpaper! If I *had* pasted my money to the wall I wouldn't have put it right by the door, would I?'

'Oh do shut up about your savings,' I said crossly. 'I'm going home.' And I walked out. She followed me to the front gate and then started shouting again: 'What about Bosun? You haven't clipped my dog. You came here under false pretences, I said I didn't like the look of you, didn't I? Well I don't . . .' One of her neighbours was spraying roses in his front garden and he gave me a cheery wink and tapped his head with his finger. 'Lost her marbles,' he said.

I don't mind lost marbles, some of our nicest acquaintances lost theirs years ago, but I do object to lost manners. I drove home looking forward to telling Brian and our friend Margaret who was coming to supper all about my crazy day.

Margaret arrived first, just back from spending a holiday with her cousin, and helped me with the supper preparations. I had cooked a casserole the previous evening so there were only the vegetables to do and the table to set. By the time everything was ready Brian still hadn't come home from work. 'He'd better have a good excuse,' I said, 'he knew you were coming tonight.' Margaret, who never gets annoyed about anything, said he'd probably had a puncture. We had another glass of plonk and waited. Then the phone rang and it was Brian to say he'd had a bit of an accident with the car and would we start dinner without him as he wasn't hungry.

'Typical,' I said, cross with relief, as I put the food on the table. 'Why does he have to have an accident today of all days?'

'Poor Brian,' said Margaret. 'It's not very nice for him to have an accident at all. Are you sure he's all right?'

'He sounded all right – he was calling from a phone box so he can't have broken anything. He said the car was a write-off though.' I was more peeved about the dinner than about the car.

'You will be sympathetic when he comes in, won't you?' said Margaret anxiously.

'Of *course* I'll be sympathetic,' I snapped. Margaret smiled to herself. When Brian came in he saw which side his bread was buttered and sat down next to Margaret.

The accident had been of the concertina variety with everyone in the line crunching in to the one in front, he explained. 'It was nearly all my fault. The chap in front signalled a right turn and I stupidly assumed he was going to make a right turn . . .' Margaret who doesn't drive, looked puzzled . . . 'then he stopped dead. I went into the back of him, the one behind went into me and so on up the line.'

'How many?'

'Five. Nobody was hurt; we weren't going fast but it was a nasty shake up.'

'Poor poor, Brian, you're shocked.' Margaret hugged him and fussed over him like a mother hen. I couldn't see why he should have two doses of sympathy especially as he'd admitted it was his fault so I went on being snappy. Margaret said she would stay the night. (She used to be a nurse and is very good at sorting people out.) 'To protect him from me, you mean?' I said.

'Well, yes, since you put it like that. You won't be able to have a row if I'm here.' Brian looked at her gratefully. I could have cheerfully throttled the pair of them and said so. But after a pot of tea we relaxed. I told them about Gwenbill and Bobjoy and the batty Mrs Land Ahoy and we made up house names from our friends' names most of which came out like Polish dissidents: Mikliz, Patrev, Vicjill.

Then Margaret told us about her holiday with her cousin Verity.

Verity had suggested a few days fishing in a Scottish loch. Margaret had envisaged relaxing by the water's edge admiring the scenery but Verity, well and truly bitten by the fishing bug, had insisted on hiring a rowing boat on the very first day. Neither of them could row. Somehow they got the boat out to the middle of the loch and Verity set up her fishing tackle. After a while both of them needed to go to the loo. Fishing *men* can pee over the edge of their boats but female anatomy isn't designed for this and the cousins had to row to the shore where there was a clump of bushes. Reaching out to the boat for a handhold Margaret lost her footing and fell overboard.

As she felt herself going down into the icy depths Margaret comforted herself with the thought that at least this would put paid to the boat outing. But she had reckoned without Verity's enthusiasm for her new hobby. 'She hauled me back into the boat, chucked me a spare anorak and *carried on fishing*.'

Brian said, 'How could she? The splash you made falling in must have driven all the fish away.' There was a silence then Margaret said to me: 'Will you bash him or shall I?'

'I'm supposed to be in shock,' Brian protested, 'Unbashable. Anyway you're a pacifist.'

'We do lapse occasionally,' Margaret assured him.

'Go on with the rowing boat story,' I said, 'Did Verity catch anything after all that excitement?'

'Mm she did. You must come and have supper with me soon, I've got some beautiful trout in the freezer.'

We packed Brian off to a hot bath and an early night

and settled down for a long natter. Having been friends since our children were small (we were near neighbours in London) there's always a lot of fat to chew over – mutual acquaintances, books we've enjoyed and, of course, our 'where did we go wrong' children.

'They could be a lot worse,' Margaret said philosophically when we eventually prepared for bed. 'At least none of them became estate agents or disc jockeys.'

'I've survived three recently,' I boasted.

'Estate agents?'

'No, disc jockeys.'

'Good heavens. Do you want to talk about it or is it too painful?'

Publishers expect their writers to do three impossible things: 1) Write bestsellers 2) Not object to the pitiful offerings that pass as dust jackets 3) Engage in unnatural practices. The last of these three is subdivided and one of the subdivisions is called book promoting. Before I explain how disc jockeys come into it perhaps I'd better run through the sequence leading up (down) to these alien creatures.

Writing a book is the easy bit. You get a big pad of paper – lined paper so that you can decipher your own handwriting later – and some comfortable pens and get on with it. The quality of the pen is crucial at this stage, anything that sticks or clogs will gum up your brain and make you irritable. A good ballpoint pen contains about five thousand words and if you lock the spare-room door and ignore dogs and husbands clamouring for clean shirts or walkies you should be getting through one or two a week. It's a very nice feeling to throw away an empty pen and pick up a full one.

When you have finished your masterpiece your troubles start. You come out of the spare room to find the hoover has rusted up and your husband has gone off with another woman so you oil one and retrieve the other. Bravely stepping on to the bathroom scales you see you've gained a stone and it's *all* on the buttocks. It's as though the billions of brain cells which you've used up in the creative process have dropped straight through to your rear. Your consternation is shared by your husband who realises this will mean weeks of nothing but salads for him too.

Having knocked your body and house back into some sort of order you re-enter the spare room for the next stage of labour – the sweaty, physically painful process of copying out your scribbles so that it's intelligible to whoever is going to type it. Next to the disc jockeys this is the worst bit. You're not creating so there's no adrenalin flow to keep you going. Fingers, shoulders and neck protest bitterly as they are forced to write out another three hundred pages. Unexpected visitors receive rapturous welcomes and every phone call is eagerly answered. ('Do tell me all about your double glazing/life insurance.') Interestingly, the telesales people can't ring off fast enough when you ask them to carry on talking. You press on with the work and one day there it is, finished. By now of course you hate the sight of it and vow never to write another word and sign on for evening classes in all the non-cerebral activities.

Then follows a shortish period of unease while the handwritten pages (no carbon copy) take their chance in the post to the typist. After this you have to keep your fingers crossed that she will remain in good health at least until your work is completed. (One typist I used to use had a nervous breakdown in the bedding department of Harrods when she came face to face with her lover's wife and I didn't get my manuscript back for four weeks.)

On then to the publishers. When they accept your offering for publication you have to go and see them on their home ground, probably so that they can make sure you're sound in wind and limb and good for a few thousand words yet. The first time I went Brian polished my shoes until they shone like conkers and I had my hair cut at a hairdresser's for the first time in ten years. The face was too daunting a repair job – years of leaving it out in all weathers had not done it a lot of good – so I left it alone and set off, apprehensively.

I thought a publisher's office would be wall to wall fluffy

carpets with concealed lighting and sophisticated secretaries telexing New York so it was an enormous relief to find it more like a vet's waiting room. There was lino on the floor of the reception area and lots of friendly girls rushing in and out like carrier pigeons with messages on pieces of paper. I'm not saying that the firm *doesn't* have electronic gadgetry but the impression was that they preferred quill pens to computers. The feeling of being at the vet's was heightened as I was shown up a flight of stairs (more lino) past some rooms which in the old days would have been family living rooms but were now partitioned off into cubicles like boarding kennels. The editor assigned to edit my manuscript led the way into her own little space which would have been barely within the legal limits of Shetland pony quarters. There were two chairs and a desk – a sort of rehearsal, I realise now, for the disc jockeys which is what all this is leading up to.

The editor who was called Esther and was just as friendly as the receptionists downstairs asked a passing carrier pigeon to bring us some coffee then we spent the morning going through the manuscript, altering bits here and there so that it would sound less like an extended letter to one's mother and more like a proper book. Although Esther had a nineteenth-century air about her and would have looked exactly right reclining on a drawing-room sofa with an adoring spaniel at her feet, she got through a prodigious amount of work. Even when her phone kept ringing she was an object lesson in how to do several things at the same time, unhurriedly dealing with the callers then returning to the work on the desk quite unruffled by the interruptions.

At lunchtime we went upstairs to a staff dining room and had a cold buffet lunch. A girl called Sheila with a gorgeous Irish brogue joined us. Sheila was in charge of publicity and had recently had to cart some awful self-centred old biddy all over Britain for book-signing sessions. I thoroughly enjoyed Sheila's wickedly funny account of the book selling trip but I began to have an uneasy feeling that a sort of scaled down version of this 'promotion' business was being planned for me.

Sure enough as soon as lunch was over Sheila whisked me in to her own kennel and roughed out an itinerary. 'We'll take a train and start at Wolverhampton,' she said, and it was like hearing the dentist telling you that next time you come you'll have to have three fillings and a new crown.

'No,' I protested. 'I can write things but I can't say things. I'd be no good at being a Someone.' Anticipating pain the safest thing to do is to switch off and hope for the best. So it was with Wolverhampton and Sheila's book promotion ideas. I can't remember a single detail of her plan apart from the fact that we would start at Wolverhampton. Mystified, she returned me to Esther who then introduced me to some more staff members and the boss himself, Mr Deutsch.

Mr Deutsch was old and very clean. He looked as though he bathed twice a day and his clothes were immaculate too; he could have been an advert for Savile Row tailoring. I can't remember what he said, only what he smelt like which was, well, expensive. On being introduced to your publisher for the first time you can hardly say, 'Cor don't you smell nice,' so instead I said I loved the smell of the building which must have sounded silly but happened to be true. I *do* get high on the distinctive smell of new books and the place was stacked with them. Mr Deutsch looked at me as if I was barmy and went away, obviously wondering to himself if he had been wise allowing Esther to take this peasant on board.

Nothing happens very fast in publishing and by the time the book was book shaped and ready for 'promotion' Sheila had left. Her successor, Helen, hadn't the same yen to go to Wolverhampton so I was spared that. Instead I was subjected to death by disc jockey which was Helen's way of working. If you are a radio addict you'll have noticed that when you move the indicator knob from Radio 4 to Radio 3 the set emits dreadful noises on the way. These come from commercial radio stations, manned by humanoids for morons. The main output from these places is that most damaging of sounds since the blitz – pop music, interspersed by weather reports, traffic news and interviews with first-time writers before they know any better.

'Piece of cake,' said Helen gaily over the phone. (We never met which was lucky for her since I don't share Esther's unflappability.) 'All you do is go along and be interviewed. I've fixed up three for you.' And she gave me the dates and times. As trustingly as an oyster I trotted along to Radio Moron number one where a girl with a clipboard was waiting to show me where to go. She had a pen dangling on a chain round her neck, the chain was so short she must have had to hold the clipboard under her chin whenever she wanted to write. She aimed me through a doorway into a cell which was much much smaller than those at the publishers. Inside the cell was a smaller one made out of perspex, like the ones you see in isolation hospitals to prevent germs from spreading. A youth sat in the inner cell playing records while in the outer casing there were several grown men fiddling with knobs on a switchboard contraption. Someone guided me into the perspex bubble and sat me down opposite the youth who removed his headphones and said, 'Hi. You'll be on in thirty-five seconds.' I wondered if a still smaller person would appear from a still smaller bubble. How on *earth* could anybody work here?

The youth replaced his headphones, threw a few switches and told his listening audience that he had here, live, a lady who had written a book and wasn't that exciting? She was here in person to tell them all about it. He said my name and pointed to a microphone in front of me. I didn't know what to say so I looked at the microphone which was the same shape as an elephant's penis. I used to work at the zoo so I know a bit about elephants. 'What do you want me to say?' I asked.

The youth hastily switched us both off and said sternly, 'We're live you know,' then he switched himself on again and told his listeners that here was the latest track from the Snotty Yobs album number fifty in the charts. By some technological magic we, in the isolation ward, didn't have to hear the record being played which I was glad about, glad too that it was taking up several minutes of 'my' air time.

'I'll ask you questions, right?' said the youth. 'When I change the record, right?'

'Right,' I said obediently. I wanted to be cooperative but I wished someone had explained the rules beforehand. The record ended and my interviewer cum disc jockey switched us on again and said brightly: 'Well now, er, Faith – what made you think of writing a book?'

There was a long silence while I considered the question. One of the men in the outer capsule mimed: 'For fuck's sake you're *live*!' and danced around in a little frenzy. I asked the youth if he had read my book and it was his turn to start sweating. He said 'I don't have time for reading.' Grabbing a copy of the book which Helen had sent him two weeks previously be began to read the blurb. That took up more minutes as he was not a fluent reader. 'Here's a good bit,' he said, desperately opening the book at random. He pushed it over the counter to me and I pushed it back again. The miming man looked as though he was going to need medical attention so I made a real effort and managed to stumble out some piffle about writing and children and pigs. In the closing seconds of the allotted time the youth picked up the book and read out the title concluding with: 'Published by Andrea Douche price of £7.95.'

When I got home I phoned Helen. She was a believer in the if-you-fall-off-get-back-on-again school of thought and sent me to the second disc jockey. The encounter was exactly the same as before, a mini hell. There you are, trapped with a boy who hasn't yet mastered joined-up writing, in a room the size of a mouse cage, expected to be witty and eloquent in between pop records. 'No more,' I said to Helen afterwards. 'Positively no more.'

'Try a phone-in,' she suggested.

'What's a phone-in?'

'You stay at home and the interviewer phones you from the studio. Sometimes the listeners phone in and ask questions.'

Naturally there were no listeners but the home-based interview was less awful than the others. I was sandwiched between reports of traffic jams at junction something or other which was a vast improvement on pop charts.

Now it was Helen's turn to leave Andrea Douche and she

was replaced by Nicky, a stunningly beautiful girl with the same strange leanings towards unknown radio stations as her predecessors. 'I've got you an hour – live,' she said. I longed for Sheila to come back and take me to Wolverhampton. 'This one's not a disc jockey,' Nicky went on. 'He's a proper interviewer. He had Alec Guinness last week.'

'He can bloody well have Alec Guinness again this week. I'm *not* interviewee material. I *can't* talk on the air and that's that.'

'Yes you can. Everybody mumbles and sweats but once you get going you'll be OK. Think of it as an hour's free advertising and it'll be fine.'

Needless to say it was not fine. The radio studio was another mouse cage and the interviewer and I disliked each other on sight. He chain-smoked Gauloises. I retaliated with Silk Cut. The two lots of smoke rose and an aerial Battle of Waterloo developed with France winning hands down. He barked out a few questions and I gasped the answers and when I peered through the fog at the clock on the wall only twenty seconds had passed. I badly wanted to inflict some physical and lasting damage on Nicky. 'Think of it as an hour's free advertising,' she had said. Huh. An hour with a charging rhino would have been more fun.

Apart from the Gauloises, the main problem was that only one of us had read the book and it was the book, so Nicky had led me to believe, that was supposed to be the subject of the interview. My opponent had the book in his possession, I could see it through the haze, but he opened the session with a monologue about a pre-war film; this lasted four lovely minutes then he asked me a question about it. As I hadn't even been born when the film was made I didn't think I was qualified to comment on it so I didn't say anything. After three adolescent disc jockeys I was getting good, not to say expert, at not saying anything. The producer of the programme exhibited the same distress signals outside the plastic cage as the producer of the previous programme. They are probably bred in large numbers in some subterranean laboratory; products of the phallic microphones and the girls with chains round their necks.

The interviewer waffled on to his listeners who by now must have numbered three - my mother, Brian's mother and Brian – all the while avoiding the eye of his rabid producer. He realised, rather late in the day, that this inert lump in front of him would not, *could* not, perform like Alec Guinness and that he would have to keep going for the best part of an hour. Although I don't think I would flip if I was trapped underground in a cave or a pothole I did flip in that plastic cage. Overcome first by a sort of lockjaw, then by a more general paralysis, I wondered dispassionately if it was physiologically possible for an entire human body to dissolve, bones and all, leaving only a pool of sweat.

There was one moment in the whole ghastly ordeal when hope flickered. The interviewer made a mistake and bowled me a short length. 'Leisure activities,' he said. 'What do you do when you're not writing?' Swift to see how something could be salvaged from this fiasco I said I worked for animal welfare, in particular the Dartmoor Livestock Protection Society, and was just going to add that that charity and the Devon Horse and Pony Sanctuary would be pleased to receive donations, when he cottoned on to what I was up to and took control again. The rest of the minutes, every one of which was made up of sixty endless seconds, eventually passed and I went home.

Brian said: 'You were *awesomely* bad, I've taped it for you,' and made me a cup of tea. I wiped the tape without playing it. The phone rang and Terry (the friend who masterminded our electrical wiring) said: 'That was horrific Faith. You were terrible but the interviewer was terrible too. These people are supposed to throw you the right questions, not make you look a complete prune. I hope you don't mind but I've taped it and I'm going to use it in my classes as an example of what not to do.' Terry was – is – the tutor – organiser for the WEA in Devon and ran classes in interviewing techniques among other things. Neither of our mothers phoned and we learned later that one had forgotten to listen and the other

94

had been unable to twiddle the right knob and had missed it.

Nicky has never mentioned radio interviews from that day to this.

Chapter Ten

'MY MUMMY SAYS frogs give you warts.' We were unloading
end-of-season plants at a late car boot sale and were too busy
to pay much attention to the small boy who was watching us.
'I kissed Conrad Onions,' he went on to nobody in particular,
'and I didn't get a wart.' His mother arranging her own stall a
couple of cars away called out: 'Don't make a nuisance of yourself, Laurence. Do you want some money for an ice cream?'

'No,' said Laurence. 'I'm working.'

'Well, work where I can keep an eye on you.' His mother
started to serve her customers and we served ours. Everything
on our stall had been reduced to 50p and we were rushed off
our feet. After an hour or so things died down and we stopped
for a breather and a cup of coffee from a thermos flask. While
we were drinking Laurence reappeared. His hands and face and
most of his shorts were black with mud. He said to Brian, 'I
need a paper bag.' Brian handed him one without comment and
he went away.

The sale was on a school football pitch which was the
usual marked-out area surrounded by longer grass next to
the hedges. Laurence's mysterious 'work' was taking place in a
ditch under one of the hedges where we could see him making
his way along on all fours. After a while he stood up holding
something carefully in the paper bag. He went back to his mother
who groaned at the sight of the mud then looked inside the paper
bag and said, 'No'.

'But Mummy . . .'

'Put it back where you found it, Laurence. You're *not*
bringing it home and that's final.'

'He's not it, he's he. He's Conrad Onions. He'll get run
over if I leave him here.'

'How can he get run over on a football pitch?'

'By a car,' said Laurence. The pitch was indisputably full of cars but his mother was unmoved. He tried again. 'By a big boy playing football. He'll get trodden on.'

'You'll get trodden on by me if you don't stop arguing. *Put it back.*'

'I'll take Laurence's frog,' I called over. 'We've got plenty more to keep it company.' Laurence was across the grass in a flash, holding out the paper bag with its precious inmate. His mother smiled gratefully and returned to her customers.

'His name's Conrad Onions,' said Laurence.

'I know, I heard you telling your mother. He'll be perfectly safe in our garden so don't worry about him. He can hibernate in our greenhouse.'

'What's hibernate?'

'It's a very long sleep. Frogs don't like the cold so they fall asleep for the whole winter.'

'For *all* the winter?' said Laurence in horror. 'But he'll miss Christmas.'

'Mm, he will. But when he wakes up in the spring he'll have a big birthday party to make up for missing Christmas.'

'When is it his birthday?'

'March. All frogs are born in March. When's yours?'

'November. I'm four and three quarters. How old are you?'

'Ninety-five.'

'How old is the flower man?'

'A hundred.'

Laurence accepted this without surprise and rummaged in the bag to say goodbye to Conrad Onions, a large frog looking rather the worse for wear after being put in a paper bag for so long. I tipped the money out of our margarine carton and replaced it with a bed of wet grass. Laurence looked round to see if his mother was watching, then guiltily kissed Conrad Onions on the nose and put him in the carton. Brian, pretending to be shocked said: 'You shouldn't do that, Laurence.'

'I don't get warts,' said Laurence airily.

'I wasn't thinking of *you*,' said Brian. 'I was feeling sorry for that poor frog catching your horrible germs. Have you seen the state you're in?' Laurence thought this was very funny and rushed back to tell his mother.

Not being frogs Brian, Anne, Marcus, Sara and I weren't able to hibernate through Christmas. Marcus hadn't intended coming home but he caught hepatitis in India and we all thought it would be wiser for him to be treated at the hospital for tropical diseases in London and then come home to rest for a while.

Before his arrival Brian and I went to our GP to find out if there were any precautions we should take against catching hepatitis from Marcus. The doctor was very matter of fact and told us there was little or no risk as long as we observed normal Western standards of hygiene. I was shaken rigid when he said calmly: 'I assume your son caught it through using infected needles?' My instinctive reaction to this was to want to leap across his desk and ram his prescription pad down his throat, luckily Brian was on hand to keep the peace. 'We don't know how he caught it,' he said, 'but it definitely wasn't through drugs.' He described Marcus to the doctor, how he was fanatically health conscious, sticking to a vegan diet and walking or swimming every day. The doctor said we were lucky. What a terrible indictment of young people as a whole, that the parents of a hepatitis patient were 'lucky' he wasn't a drug addict.

Marcus, stepping off the train at Exeter, was thin and yellow: 'I've been much yellower than this, it's nearly worn off now,' he said.

'You look awful. What did they sat at the hospital?'

'They wormed me. I had three different sorts of stomach worms. I can't remember the names but one sort was—'

'We don't want the details,' Brian interrupted. 'What did they say about the hepatitis?'

'Nothing much. It's the mild one. You won't catch it as long as I have my own towel and we all wash properly – the usual stuff.'

'But how did you catch it in the first place?' I said. 'You're always careful to wash your food, aren't you?'

'Of course I am. I must have caught it off an old man I met. He lives in a hovel, you couldn't imagine how poor he is. He sleeps on a heap of rags and craps on the floor in one corner. It's really dreadful, flies everywhere. He hasn't got any friends.'

'He wouldn't have if he lives in an open sewer. Whatever made you go into such a place?'

'He was lonely. People leave food in the doorway but nobody ever goes inside. I hadn't the heart to say no when he invited me in.' The old man had pressed Marcus to have a drink with him and Marcus, thinking he could somehow dispose of it when the old man wasn't looking, had accepted. 'He'd rigged up a still,' Marcus went on. 'The stuff was *lethal* – pure alcohol. Made out of vegetable peelings, I think.'

'You *drank* it?' Brian said incredulously.

'Only one or two swallows. It was real firewater, I forced a bit down just to be friendly but it made me choke. The next day I was ill with the Dreaded Lurgi and a week after that I went down with hepatitis.'

'I don't suppose he ever washed the glasses?' I said.

'Glasses? He's got one enamel plate and one kind of basin thing for drinking out of. We shared the basin . . .'

Sara meanwhile had taken a temporary job in London driving diplomats' children to and from school and also on educational outings. She found the rich spoilt kids utterly depressing. 'They've nothing to look forward to,' she said. 'Nothing. By the time they're ten they've already done everything and been everywhere – winter sports holidays, cruises, flights on Concorde – they have so much pocket money it's coming out of their ears and do you know what? They're miserable.' She had watched them once in a safari park, bored to death because they had all been to leisure parks in California which were bigger and better. On the coach home she had heard them playing some sort of betting game, the stakes being their Parker Pens and Swiss watches. It was a far cry from a game of conkers in the playground and from Marcus's old man crapping on the floor of his hut.

Christmas was a culinary free-for-all. None of us liked turkey but the dogs (five of them this year) and the two cats did. So the animals had turkey, Brian and Sara had steak, Anne and I had crab and Marcus had a field day lecturing us all on our evil ways. A vegan with hepatitis is not in the strongest position to extol the virtues of healthy living but Marcus, to his credit, stuck to his guns.

Preferring to cook for himself he grilled some raw carrots a day or two later, not a dish that is likely to find its way into gourmet recipe books. To accompany the carrots he decided on Indian pancakes. He mixed some flour and water together then kept adding more flour until he had a substance that *Blue Peter* viewers would have been familiar with. The rest of us stood around watching with interest to see what he would do next.

'They cook these on hot stones in the south,' he said. We were running low on hot stones so I handed him a frying pan and a bottle of vegetable oil. He said he didn't need the oil and put the dry frying pan on the stove. I said anxiously: 'Marcus, you *do* need oil.' Anne and Sara backed me up. The kitchen filled with the smell of hot metal. Marcus dolloped some of his mixture into the pan where it immediately went black on the underside. He turned it over and it went black on the other side. Brian opened the kitchen door to let some of the smoke out. 'That's very odd,' said Marcus. 'It never does that in India.' By now the adhesive properties of flour and water paste were only too apparent. Marcus blamed it on the frying pan, 'It must be aluminium,' he said waving the burnt offering above his head like a censer. As I never use aluminium for cooking and had taught both children not to, that was too much. 'You know perfectly well it's cast iron,' I said. 'Now will you please put that charred mess in the garden to cool off and come and eat.'

'No, I'll get it right next time. I'll alter the mixture. I wish I could show you how the Indian women do it on a hot stone.'

Sara said if she had a hot stone handy she would drop it on his head. Two frying pans later Marcus admitted defeat and made do with a Marks and Spencer ready prepared dish of broccoli and asparagus in a mushroom sauce. The Christmas holiday passed.

Unimpressed by Marcus's enthusiasm for Eastern philosophy and cuisine, Sara returned to London where she was planning to start her own business selling 'seconds' of pure wool sweaters on a market stall. Marcus said darkly: 'She'll get pneumonia standing in Camden Town market all winter.' He would have liked us all to go back to India with him and become existentialists; he couldn't understand why we didn't want to. Somewhat disgruntled with us all he went to stay with Anne in Totnes for a week which he enjoyed very much especially when he discovered a colony of vegans squatting in a disused ruin. (Some said it wasn't a ruin before the colony moved in, but that might have been another example of the them and us feeling in the town.) As well as the vegans Marcus met a reincarnation of a Russian prince and a girl who offered to read his bumps. Unlike a lot of soothsayers this one made a charge for her services (£4.50) and Marcus declined, saying he had already had his entrails read free at the hospital for tropical diseases.

However he didn't want to leave Totnes without trying out something in the alternative line so on the principle of 'When in Rome . . .' he and Anne took up finger eating. This is exactly what it sounds like: you abandon knives and forks in favour of fingers. It's supposed to be good for improving your powers of concentration while at the same time keeping you in harmony with your body. Anne, who is always receptive to new ideas, entered into the spirit of the thing while Marcus was staying with her but had to report that there was no improvement in their powers of concentration at all. She said it saved on the washing up and the dogs loved to join in but as a mental stimulant she would stick to crosswords.

If Marcus hadn't booked his plane ticket back to India I think he might have stayed longer in Totnes. He was fascinated by all the different therapies on offer. Properly trained healers in fields such as osteopathy, homoeopathy, Alexander technique, aromatherapy, reflexology and the rest advertised their services

101

on neatly printed cards in health-shop windows. Alongside these cards were those of cults like Turnip Worshippers and Cosmic Connectors. Their cards were handwritten, sometimes quite beautifully, and decorated with little pieces of pressed vegetation which decayed and fell off in time. Symbolic?

'It's all so *silly*,' Marcus said. 'It gives the real healers a bad name.' He was quite nonplussed by the groups that charged participants an arm and a leg for sitting on the floor in a fog of cannabis. This sort of escapism has always puzzled us too. Pot smokers are the first to go on about how wonderful it is just to exist, and how privileged they feel to be parts of Nature (as though the rest of us were parts of a motorbike), then they contradict themselves by deliberately dulling the very senses nature has given them.

One of the esoteric societies seemed to be a sort of astral travel agency. Members were taught how to zoom off to wherever they fancied without all the bother of taking their bodies with them. As a method of cheap travel one could see the advantages; also it must save a lot of hassle not having to find a neighbour to mind the cat and not having to cancel the milk. But I wouldn't have thought it would be much of a holiday – no suntan, no snapshots, no new friends unless you count other disembodied souls on the same trip. And what of the body left at home? What would it get up to in its soul's absence? Worst of all, what would happen if your soul *liked* its new found freedom and refused to come back to your boring old body? There you'd be, stuck on automatic pilot, with the shopping and housework as usual, while your soul was living it up with some astral Lothario in Benidorm. On balance, and despite the expense of road and rail travel, separate holidays sound much too complicated to be worth the trouble.

Turnip worship was another alternative pastime that Marcus found fault with. According to him, the real turnip worshippers wouldn't recognise the watered-down form as practised in Devon. When he said this we thought the hepatitis must have got to his brain. He was offended. 'Look it up if you don't believe me.' Not wishing to be the laughing stock at our local library we sorted through our own books and to our astonishment found a reference to holy turnips in an essay written by the late and very lamented James Cameron.

Travelling through Nepal, Cameron had come across a remote Tibetan temple lit by butter-lamps. The lamas invited him in and showed him their wall decorations which included a painting depicting the ritual of Glorious Offerings. One of these holy offerings was the turnip and there was also something called intestinal concretions but Cameron doesn't say exactly what that meant.

'Told you so,' said Marcus smugly. 'I've *been* there, you see.'

'You said it was turnip *worship*,' I reminded him. 'James Cameron only mentions turnips as holy offerings.' We argued over this and read the Cameron essay aloud and Brian looked at us open-mouthed, thinking we were making it up as we went along. Marcus handed him the book and he checked the story for himself. 'If it wasn't James Cameron I still wouldn't believe it,' he said. 'Whoever heard of a holy turnip?'

Marcus said the monks had to do something in the long winter evenings. 'They don't have television or radio and they're cut off for months at a time by the snow. So they're into turnips.'

When he was well again he returned to globe-trotting, promising to take better care of himself in future. We try not to worry too much about his safety but it's not easy. He always seems to be in the vicinity of trouble; not in the thick of it, thank goodness, but near enough to make us anxious. There was the storming of the Golden Temple, the assassination of Mrs Gandhi, the Bhopal Chemical disaster and latterly the typhoon in the Philippines. Marcus was in the areas of all these when they were happening. When he went to Japan to earn some money we weren't in the least bit surprised when we opened a newspaper and read a headline on the financial pages: YEN COLLAPSES. Brian said: 'It would, it saw him coming.'

Chapter Eleven

DURING THE WINTER months our cowslips stood dormant under cold glass and very healthy they looked, lined up in neat blocks, five hundred to a block. Brian used part of the rest of the glasshouses to bring on Universal pansies and I used another part to hang the washing out. The pansies were a comparatively new variety which flowered all winter. We planted some up in ornamental tubs outside our sitting-room window, it was nothing short of miraculous to watch them recover from a hard overnight frost. By midday they would have shaken off the frost crystals and be standing upright in full bloom, turning their sweet kitten faces towards the sunlight. As yet they were not all that well known which was a pity since there can't be many things as uplifting as a clump of pansies in bloom, especially in January. We sold most of our stock to friends and some to garden/pet shops. Joe Public as a whole simply didn't believe pansies could flower all winter; if I'd been the plant researcher responsible for breeding them I think I would have crawled into a corner and quietly cut my throat.

But the cowslips were quite popular. People would buy them for all sorts of different reasons – an evocation of a country childhood, a wish to put back into the environment what 'progress' had taken out, a fancy for old-time wine making, all sorts of things. Ours were 25p a plant and we sold a thousand or so in dribs and drabs, twenty here half a dozen there, it mounted up. At this stage they were still dormant so what people were buying was a promise, as you do with a packet of seed.

As the days lengthened we had to space the cowslips out to accommodate their expanding girths. Tiny buds appeared deep in the heart of each plant and looking after them took up many tedious hours a week. They had to be fed and watered more or less individually as we didn't have any modern technology in the old glasshouses. Brian ordered the season's seedlings – geraniums, fuchsias and begonias, the same mix as the previous year – and while we waited for these to be delivered we wondered what on earth we were going to do with all the surplus cowslips. Growing so many to start with had been a bad mistake. Our outlets were very limited, it was closed season for car boot sales, and we came to the reluctant decision that if we hadn't sold them by the time the other plants came we would dump them.

The patron saint of cowslips intervened. One morning the phone rang and a man's voice said: 'I wonder if you can help me? I *must* have two thousand cowslip plants by Saturday.'

Well. We had often wondered what it must feel like to win the pools. Now we knew.

'Tell me again.' Brian prised the phone receiver from my hand and replaced it reverently. 'A man said what?'

'He said he must have two thousand cowslip plants by Saturday. Heavy emphasis on the must.'

'But who was he? What did he sound like?'

'He rang off. I said he could have them for 20p as it's a bulk order and he said he would collect them tomorrow afternoon. Then he rang off.'

As we parcelled up the plants into boxes of fifty we speculated about the buyer. Was he doing it for a bet? Had he proposed to a girl who said I'll only marry you if you can find me two thousand cowslips by Saturday? Perhaps he was an elf obeying orders from his fairy king to smarten up a few woodland glades. Would he pay in fairy gold?

When he came the following afternoon we had made so many guesses about his urgent need for cowslips we deliberately didn't ask him the real reason. As far as we were concerned he was a whimsical being on a whimsical errand and anything more prosaic would only spoil the magic. He paid in coin of the realm (our realm) and drove off in a lorry that left deep tyre marks in our mud. Brian, who is not very good at folklore, said accusingly, 'He didn't even have pointed ears.'

That was *still* not the end of the cowslip saga. Between us we and our nursery-owning friends Raymond and Valerie had sold or given away the best part of six thousand plants. This included the tail-enders which each of us had planted in our own gardens to be rid of them. It was just as well that we had kept some back otherwise we would have thought that our customers had suddenly become colour-blind. The first indication that something was wrong – perhaps 'wrong' is putting it too strongly – was when someone rang up to say he thought cowslips were yellow. Brian took the call and I heard him say: 'Yes, that's right, yellow. There are some cultivated strains which come out red but wild cowslips are yellow . . . did you say pink? . . . semi-double, eh? . . . sounds pretty . . . no I wasn't being facetious but I don't really know what you're talking about . . . O.K. I'll see what I can do. Bye.'

'What was all that about?' I said.

'Some chap complaining that one of his cowslips is pink. It's probably a weed.'

'Why did you say you'd see what you could do?'

He shrugged. 'Don't know. It's automatic.' We put the call out of our minds but the next time we passed one of our cowslip patches in the garden we glanced at it, blinked and stopped dead. For instead of a sheet of yellow heads nodding in the breeze as per gardening books there was a sheet of *multi-coloured* heads nodding, etc. 'Oh my God,' said Brian. 'They've crossed over.'

One thing that can be said about gardening is that it's seldom dull. 'What does crossed over mean?' I asked.

Brian pointed to a bed of polyanthus and primulas some distance from the parent cowslips. I pictured them heaving their little roots out of the soil and marching lecherously over to the cowslip patch. Brian said, 'It's not funny. You've let your cowslips breed with the primulas.' (Note how they immediately become 'yours' now that they had been naughty. The same goes for the dogs if they're sick on the carpet.)

Technically speaking my cowslips had committed allogamy

or cross-fertilization with plants of the same genetic make-up as themselves. In lay terms (which seems appropriate) if plant A doesn't like the look of the chap in the same bed she can have a word with a cooperative insect and arrange a union with the more fanciable plant B who might – and in this case did – live yards away. Providing the object of her affections comes from a suitable family the couple will be blessed with hundreds of bastard offspring.

No wonder then that the seed had germinated so exceptionally well. As every mongrel owner knows, crossbreeds are hardier, healthier, longer lived and more prolific than their pedigree cousins. 'They're gorgeous,' I said. 'I don't care if they're not pure.'

'*You* might not but what about the people who bought them? They expect cowslips to be cowslips not some rainbow freaks.'

Primroses, primulas, polyanthus, cowslips and oxslips all come from the same family – primula. Selective breeding has produced all sorts of colour combinations including many stripy ones and some with deckle-edged petals. These are confined to just the polyanthus and primulas, or rather they were until my cowslips turned so promiscuous.We even had a *green* one.

When we asked Raymond if any of his customers had complained about coloured cowslips he laughed. 'As soon as I had the first complaint I guessed what had happened,' he said. 'You must have put the parent plants too near some polys or prims.'

'I did,' I admitted. 'I'd no idea they were closely related. But what did you say to the customers, Ray?'

'Oh,' he said airily, 'I told them that these were special varieties. Any fool can grow a *yellow* cowslip, can't they?'

As their nursery – Hill House – is only a few miles from Totnes it seemed to me little short of inspirational to make a virtue out of the plants' freakishness. In a way it was a pity we didn't have any left to sell, I would have enjoyed doing an Alternative Cowslip label.

At the time Raymond and Valerie were running two weekly

market stalls in addition to their own nursery. Valerie asked us if we would like to take over one of the stalls as they couldn't really spare the time to man both. We jumped at the chance of another outlet particularly as the rent was only 50p. When we told Sara she said she couldn't believe you could get a stall for that. The rent of her market stall was twenty-four pounds a day but then hers was in London and ours was in what estate agents call a rural idyll. (Spelt idle if the estate agent is employing YTS typists.)

At first we didn't have nearly enough of our own stuff to make a nice display so we arranged to sell Raymond and Valerie's for them on one half of the stall and ours on the other half. Now the stall looked lovely stacked with tiers of polyanthus, cinerarias and pansies interspersed with the greenery of container grown conifers. At the front we placed buckets of cut pinks which Valerie picked and bunched fresh every morning. Sometimes customers would ask for a named variety and we had to bone up on all sixty of the named pinks which they grew at the nursery.

We were amused on one occasion when an old lady, a true Devonian, asked for 'Two bunches of they pretty Little Jack Horner.' There was no such variety and we assumed, correctly, that the customer meant Old Mother Hubbard. This was a new pink which Raymond, whose surname is Hubbard, had bred and named himself. (This was awarded a highly commended in the Royal Horticultural Society trials.) Brian said, 'I think you mean Old Mother Hubbard,' and wrapped a couple of bunches for her. She showed the flowers to one of her cronies. 'Look Ethel,' she said, 'aren't they pretty? They'm called Little Miss Muffet.'

But we hadn't seen the last of her yet. I had put some paperback copies of my first two books to sell on the stall. The old lady might not even have noticed them but a chatty customer pointed them out to her and told her I'd written them. 'What for?' she said. However, she bought the first book and the following week made a beeline for the stall. 'Very satisfactory,' she said, prodding the books with a forefinger. 'I'll take the next one.' Another week went by and there she was again. I wondered if I would get another school-report type of comment. This time, however, she prodded me not the book as if I was a cauliflower. 'Not stupid – not stupid at all. I'll have the third one now.'

I said 'I'm sorry, I'm afraid the third one isn't in paperback yet. You can get a hardback from the library though.'

'I'll wait until you'm got a thin one. I only likes the thin ones.'

The Green Lanes project ended and the workforce disbanded. Brian couldn't make up his mind whether to get another job or stay at home and concentrate on our own growing so, being a Gemini, he did both. He went to work for Raymond at the nursery part-time and spent his leisure hours having a busman's holiday in our greenhouses.

Hill House Nursery, Landscove, Nr. Totnes – I put that in so people wanting some of the Hubbards' excellent mail-order pinks can write direct to them and not to me – used to be a vicarage. It was owned at one time by the gardening writer Edward Hyams who laid out the grounds in part neo-classical style and then wrote books about how he did it, the same as Vita Sackville-West and Sissinghurst. When Raymond and Valerie bought the place in 1981 the grounds had gone back to nature so, with the aid of Hyams' own book, *The Englishman's Garden*, they set about recreating his original garden design. They had their nearly adult children still living at home but even so rumour had it that by the time the heavy work was finished even their osteopath needed an osteopath.

When we first met them we had only recently moved to the area and didn't know very much about Totnes or the alternative movement. One day we were having a cup of tea with Valerie and their youngest daughter Judith who was home from college, chatting about this and that when in came Raymond. 'I've been assaulted,' he said and reached for the teapot. (Do all growers rely so heavily on tea?) Nobody reacted with much more than a raised eyebrow or two. 'Raped then,' continued Raymond, determined to get a better response.

The trouble was, he is such a big burly man, the exact opposite of Valerie who darts about like a little minnow, that it was hard to imagine him in any sort of physical danger.

'*You've* been raped?' said Valerie, making it sound as if it was usually someone else this happened to. 'Do you want a biscuit?'

'I thought you were going to the bank,' said Judith. Brian said encounters with bank managers often seemed like rape and Raymond said no it hadn't happened in the bank but in the street outside. 'I got caught up in a demo,' he said. 'An all female demo. I wouldn't have minded so much if they'd been saving something worthwhile, like toads, but . . .'

'They did toads in March,' interrupted Judith helpfully.

'Yes I know and as I say I wouldn't mind being caught up in a pro-toad rally but this was a ban-the-loo-roll mob.'

'Ban the *loo roll*?' we chorused. 'In favour of what or shouldn't we ask?' Our imaginations boggled. Judith said was that why demonstrators so often wore army camouflage trousers and Valerie said, 'Judith!'

'In favour of recycled loo rolls,' said Raymond. Our imaginations boggled some more but it was not as bad as it sounded. The villains in this demo were coloured loo rolls which, it was alleged, are dyeing the oceans pink and yellow and upsetting marine life. The demonstrators wanted everyone to stop buying the coloured ones and insist on white only. The ideal product in their opinion was the loo roll made out of recycled paper like egg boxes but if these were unacceptable (a later trial proved them to be much too similar to egg boxes) then plain white was the next best thing.

'Sounds laudable enough,' I said. 'After all if everyone stopped using detergents and stuck to bio-degradables we could cut down river pollution. It may be the same with loo rolls.'

'They may have *meant* well but they didn't have to be so rough,' said Raymond.

Brian said in surprise, 'Rough? Totnes hippies rough?'

'Who said anything about hippies? These were middle-aged

and elderly *women*, Brian, in full cry. I nearly got knocked down in the crush.'

Valerie burst our laughing and said she would never have believed that Raymond would object to being crushed by a crowd of women. To which Raymond answered that these weren't women, they were more like a horde of Amazons. Then he described how they had joined hands, formed a line and swept everyone in their way along like so many leaves. It got so bad that the traffic warden had to radio for help.

'How did the traffic warden come into it?' asked Brian, 'was he a yellow Andrex supporter?'

'They all lay down in rows across the street,' continued Raymond, 'and nothing could get by. There was a traffic jam a mile long.'

'Oh I know the ones you mean now,' said Judith. 'They did that for Nelson Mandela.'

'They're a busy lot then,' said Raymond. 'Toads, Nelson Mandela, organically grown loo rolls ... Anyway they wouldn't budge for the traffic warden so he went away. Then the police arrived in full strength – all two of them – and one of the coppers told the demo leader that if she didn't move her lot out of the road he'd have to miss his lunch hour.'

And this apparently had done the trick. The women, most of whom were mothers and grandmothers, couldn't bear the thought of a young constable going back to work on an empty stomach so they called it a day. I was glad to learn that the alternative movement even extended to alternative policing – much more civilised than batons and tear gas.

Fox hunting was another activity that involved protesters. It used to be a pastime for rich people only but nowadays anybody can join in. It is not unusual to see a hunt involving first the fox, then the hounds, then the mounted followers. In hot pursuit come the hunt saboteurs, followed by the police, followed by the press, followed by the neutral observers. Everyone has a wonderful day out in the fresh air and nobody that matters – i.e. the fox – gets hurt. Foxes in some regions are said to be getting so good at recognising their supporters that they will circle round and rejoin the *back* of the crowd where they know they will be perfectly safe. A useful spin off from this new-style spectator sport is the extra business it brings to mobile catering vans; they load up with an extra few dozen hot pasties and do a roaring trade at half-time. And although we haven't seen this for ourselves we've heard that at the end of the day foxes will return to the mobile van sites to eat the leftover chips and things that the kindly drivers have put out for them.

One person who always kept a wary eye open for the law was Mrs Curtis, known in her circle as the Poaching Granny. Poachers normally come in large sizes and are male and muscular but Mrs Curtis was none of these things. She was the archetypal 'little old lady' which may explain why she was so successful as a part-time felon. It all started with patchwork cushion covers. Mrs Curtis was a skilled needlewoman and had supplemented her old-age pension for some years by selling patchwork to her local craft shop. During the summer she liked to take her materials to a nearby reservoir and sit by the water's edge as she worked. Fishermen would come over and chat to her and through them she learned quite a lot about trout – their life cycle, feeding habits and so forth; also about the life cycle and feeding habits of the local water bailiff. All this was merely academic until she realised that trout were fetching interestingly high prices. . .

So she had a think did naughty old Mrs Curtis and after her think she went to a library well away from her own village and settled down to some serious studying. She then invested in a rod and line plus – masterly touch – a huge brand new wicker fishing basket which could be seen a mile off. She also bought a yearly season ticket and a few day licences to launch her new career on a wholly legal footing. She was now entitled to catch and to keep up to four trout in any one day. The stage was set.

For the first few weeks she was careful not to catch any fish and the water bailiff on his daily patrol would stop by and pull her leg about the empty basket. After a while he even forgot to ask to see her day licence and Mrs Curtis, safe in her Miss Marple disguise, was happy to let him humour her. She carried on sewing patchwork cushion covers by the reservoir, leaving her fishing rod trailing in the water like any sloppy amateur.

Fishing purists will have to skip the next bit.

Having established herself as a slightly dotty old lady who sewed and fished at the same time, Mrs Curtis then embarked on stage two of her plan. She baited up with brandlings. (The ban on using worms for game fishing isn't because of pressure from worm welfare groups but because catching trout on a worm is too easy. It's unsporting and therefore Not Done.) Soon she was hauling in as many trout as her sewing bag would hold. Once or twice a week she would draw the friendly bailiff's attention to her new fishing basket and make him admire the solitary fish inside which she had caught 'by a fluke' even occasionally getting him to help carry her basket up the bank. She never asked him to carry her sewing bag, the weight of which would have given him a hernia, nor did she tell him that she had sold her small freezer and bought a bigger one. Her coffee mornings grew in popularity.

Chapter Twelve

BRIAN ENJOYED WORKING at the nursery (no responsibility when it's someone else's nursery) and I enjoyed the continued freedom of days on end without lunches. On the whole I like men, they remind me of puppies, but there's one thing I don't like about them and that is their inability to go without lunch. Women on their own at home grab something from the fridge when they're hungry, top it up with a couple of bananas and that's it – no trouble, no washing up. Among my own friends I can't think of a single exception to this rule. Stay-at-home men will say, 'But we only have soup and salad, what's so difficult about that?' and they're right, up to a point. It's not *difficult* to make soup or salad but it's a nuisance to have to stop what you're doing in order to prepare a meal you don't even want. So, having the lord and master off the premises during the week was a very good thing. Ironically, his packed lunches were far nicer than anything I ever gave him at home. I think I felt so guilty at being glad to see the back of him that I would go to endless trouble to make the packed meals really interesting.

As the number of my dog customers grew so did our transport problems. When Brian had been green laning his hours had been eight-thirty to five-thirty. If I needed the car I would drive him to work and collect him and this left a good stretch of working day for me. But at Hill House he only worked from nine to three as he wanted time to see to things at home. We thought about getting a motorbike but Devon's far from dry weather decided us against it and we continued as before. In the mornings we would synchronise our watches, an act of optimism rather than efficiency, almost as though the doing of it would somehow make the day run more smoothly. 'I wish you'd synchronise your bloody dogs,' Brian grumbled when I sometimes turned up to collect him at four o'clock, five o'clock and even, on one occasion, six o'clock. (A hostile poodle had tried to have me for lunch and I finished up in Casualty. The owner gave me a *thirty pence* tip for 'the extra trouble'.) But if you work with animals the one thing you can't do is watch the clock, nor would I ever want to. I charge by the dog not by the hour and if some take twice as long as others that's fine by me. Even in cash terms this policy pays off. In one neighbourhood alone I poached fifteen dogs from another mobile dog lady who was reputed to work so fast she left clipper burns on her customers' skins. My dogs might die of boredom but at least they never get hurt.

A friend once asked me why I didn't work from home. 'Get the owners to bring the dogs to your place,' she said. 'You've got the spare room and it would save all that driving.' Brian gave a yelp of horror and I told my friend a cautionary tale . . .

When I was twenty-one I had a brilliant idea. I would board cats while their owners were on holiday. It would be a 'home from home' service with the cats living as part of the family instead of being shut away in horrid little cages as they were in commercial catteries.

A postcard in a local pet-shop window soon brought results and a steady stream of Tiddles and Biggles and Fluffs signed in. All went more or less according to plan until I got over-confident and booked in eight cats all at once. We had a large Victorian house with stacks of rooms so there was no reason for the cats to quarrel but they did. They would growl and hiss and spit, then lash out at each other in passing. Great chunks of fur began to appear on the stairs which was where they all liked to congregate and I worried about what the owners would say when they found a houseful of bald cats. I nailed some wire mesh over the windows in a top-floor room so that I could safely leave the windows open, then I put four cats in there and shut the door. The other four were shut in the kitchen where I could keep an eye on them and nip their fights in the bud. It wasn't exactly living as part of the family but I thought it might cut down their actual injuries if they had separate quarters.

When I went upstairs to feed the top-floor cats three came over to purr and rub themselves against my legs. The relief at finding them not fighting was replaced by anxiety then panic. The fourth cat had vanished.

It must have been the wire mesh I thought as I shut the windows and rushed downstairs. Probably a hole somewhere . . . oh *hell*, why didn't I do it properly? I checked in the cat register notebook to find out which cat had gone: 'Sooty Beardsley, Cranley Gardens, N.10. Jet black, no white markings, 3 yrs old, neutered. Hates Kit e Kat, try sardines if he gets fussy. Owners away 2 weeks.' There was also Sooty's vet's telephone number. Fat lot of good if poor Sooty got run over and killed. I closed the book and did what most girls of twenty-one do in a crisis. I phoned my mother.

'Lost a cat? No of course it won't come back of its own accord, not to your house. Does it live very far away? Oh well, that sounds hopeful. Go round to its own house and wait for it there. How on earth should I know whether it'll get run over? How are the babies? Don't snap my head off, I only asked . . .'

Marcus was fifteen months old at the time and Sara four weeks. I chucked them both into Sara's pram, Marcus protesting loudly as was his habit, and walked through the busy streets to Sooty's house. Every time a car braked I had heart failure expecting to see a squashed cat under the wheels.

Sooty was in the Beardsleys' front garden calmly watching the world go by. Cautiously I parked the pram and crept up on him. To my surprise, instead of running off the way he did in our house he came towards me purring and let me pick him up. I hadn't remembered to bring a cat basket so I wrapped him in Sara's blanket and stuffed him down into the pram with the babies. Sara woke up cold and started to cry, Marcus came out in sympathy and suddenly I had second thoughts about boarding cats.

116

When we got home I left the babies unattended in the street and took Sooty indoors first. (A friend of mine did something similar once. She had forgotten her key so she laid her newborn-baby down on the front step while she climbed in through a loo window. By a very unlucky chance her health visitor chose that very moment to call.) They were still bawling their heads off when I fetched them but nobody reported me, maybe my lucky day after all. I strapped Marcus into his high chair and gave him some food to hurl about while I fed Sara. Peace reigned for a while although I did have a fleeting feeling that something was wrong. All five cats in the kitchen – the four original ones plus Sooty – were eating Kit e Kat and not fighting. Never one to look a gift horse in the mouth I accepted the situation without giving it a second thought.

After I had put Sara down for a sleep I showed Marcus how to eat like a human being and later, when the battleground had been cleared up, Marcus said suddenly: 'Pussy's up a sky.'

'Marcus – you said a *sentence*. Aren't you *clever*? Say it again.'

'Pussy's up a sky.'

'Marvellous. It's not all that accurate but it's a very impressive first sentence. I expect you mean pussy's down the well, it's the same rhythm. Try pussy's down the well.'

Over the next two days we tried Marcus on every conceivable permutation of cats and active verbs. When they weren't sitting on mats they were going to London to see the queen or following in the wake of the pied piper. He was not interested. Higher education could wait. 'Pussy's up a sky,' he insisted. Obstinacy was, and has remained Marcus's strong suit.

On the evening of the second day following the first utterance of his precious sentence I was carrying him upstairs when he struggled free and pointed to the skylight in the roof. 'Pussy's up a *sky*,' he shouted at the top of his voice. I looked up just in time to see a worried black face peering down through the glass. 'God almighty!' I shrieked and dumped him quickly in his cot before running for the loft ladder. 'Mighty mighty,' Marcus echoed. He must have thought it was going to be a hard life growing up in a place where it took two days to get a simple message across.

As I struggled down the ladder with Sooty Beardsley mark one threatening death and destruction to all cat minders, everything began to make sense. No wonder Sooty had seemed a reformed character – his sudden liking for Kit e Kat and his friendly behaviour weren't due to a change of heart but to a change of cat. Mighty mighty indeed. But how had the real Sooty got on the roof? I shut him in the kitchen, where he immediately started a fight, and went upstairs to the top cats' room. It didn't take long to discover the escape route. I had forgotten to board up the fireplace. Luckily the other cats weren't as bright as Sooty and all three were still with us.

Getting Sooty the Second back to his own home was far harder than kidnapping him because he didn't want to be left and kept following me along the street. I was a nervous wreck by the time I got away, any moment I thought the owner would appear and demand an explanation.

Ten days later when Mr and Mrs Beardsley came to collect their cat they said he looked different and I thought for one heart-stopping moment that I'd switched the wrong cat. 'He's thinner,' said Mrs Beardsley. 'I expect he missed us. Has he been a good boy?' I nodded. She bent down and ruffled Marcus's hair. 'And what's your name darling?'

'Sara,' said Marcus.

'He's not talking yet,' I said hurriedly. 'Well, only gibberish.' No bolt of lightning struck and Marcus didn't have the means to defend himself so everything ended up all right. But not knowing when he might make his next leap forward into sentences was too nerve-racking and I stopped boarding cats when the holiday season ended.

Another good reason for working away from home is that you meet some very interesting people. If all my Bens and Ruffs and Rosies had come to me I would never have learned (a) how to shorten curtains without hemming (b) how to embalm a corpse and (c) how to stop a cockatoo getting homesick. I will skip the embalming because although I find pathology fascinating I

118

realise that it's not everyone's cup of tea but I will pass on the curtains and cockatoo tips.

One of my customers was a poodle called Benjamin Illingworth, rather a mouthful but then one doesn't often address a dog in full. The owner, Mrs Illingworth, was an elderly widow with tremendous artistic flair – visiting the house was always a treat – but was hopeless at sewing. She loved going to jumble sales and would stagger home laden with things like patchwork quilts and wicker hampers which she flung around the house seemingly at random but actually with such skill that you wondered how the old sofa had looked before it had its new cover and where the logs had been stored before the hamper arrived.

I'd finished clipping Benjamin one morning when she called me into the dining room to admire her latest bargain, a set of green velvet curtains faded to a lovely subtle lichen colour. 'How much do you think I gave for these?' she said, holding them up to the window.

'Oh at least a fiver, that green is wonderful, isn't it?' I felt quite green myself – with envy.

'Twenty pence.'

'I don't know how you do it,' I said.

'Sometimes it's best to go right at the end. You can often knock them down – these curtains had been marked at a pound – because they want to get rid of everything. I'm glad you like them, they'll look nice in here, won't they?'

'They will if they fit.' Then I had an idea. 'If they don't fit I'll give you a pound for them.'

The lure of big profits didn't tempt her. 'I'll make them fit. Have you got time to give me a hand?'

'Me? I'm afraid I'm even worse at sewing than you are.'

'Oh, you won't have to sew anything,' she said. 'I'll show you.' Climbing onto a chair she held one of the curtains up to the window. It was too short.

'It's too short,' I said eagerly. 'I'll give you one fifty.'

Mrs Illingworth ignored this and asked me to measure the gap at the bottom. 'Use a ruler. I want to know exactly.'

Mystified I measured between the window sill and the bottom

of the curtain. 'Two and a quarter inches. I see your ruler hasn't gone metric.'

She laughed. 'It never will. I shall also continue to cook in ounces and think in real money. Could you hand me the screw-driver, please.' With practised skill she unscrewed the curtain rail then with a bradawl she made some new screw holes two and a quarter inches below the old ones. After she had fixed the rail into its new position the curtains fitted exactly and the whole job had taken no more than ten minutes.

I said: 'What do you do if the curtains are too long. Surely then you'd have to take up the hem?'

'No,' she said, 'I never touch the bottoms if they've been nicely done, I'd only ruin them. I always chop from the top then neaten up their jagged ends with glue.'

I said she sounded like a *Blue Peter* graduate. 'Wonderful programme,' she replied, 'I never miss it.'

So that's tip number one – if you want to shorten curtains move the rail and leave the hems alone. When I think of all the *miles* of hemming I must have done over the years I could kick myself for not having thought of it. Tip number two – how to cure a homesick cockatoo – hasn't the same every day application but you never know when it might come in useful.

The cockatoo was called Shane. He belonged to a bachelor who suddenly fell ill with appendicitis and had to go to hospital before he had had time to make arrangements for Shane. A nice neighbour, Mrs Herring, took the bird into her own home as she thought he would get cold in an empty house but poor Shane couldn't take the double shock of a missing owner and a change of home. He turned his face to the wall and pined. He wouldn't touch his food or water and Mrs Herring was very worried in case he died while he was in her care.

I met Shane when I went to the Herring household to clip their dog Flopsy. (Some people never *think* when they name their puppies, fancy being called Flopsy Herring.) I was working at one end of the kitchen while Mrs Herring did some ironing at the other end. She had her radio on and was listening to Scarlatti. It wasn't until I switched off my electric clippers that

I heard some not so classical music coming from the sitting room. It clashed most horribly with the Scarlatti. 'What's that noise?' I said.

'Country and Western,' said Mrs Herring. 'I have to have it on for Shane.'

'Shane?' I'd never heard her refer to her grandson before and was surprised she didn't ask him to turn it down a bit.

'Next door's cockatoo.'

'With his *own radio*?'

'Cassettes actually,' said Mrs Herring. Then she told me about her neighbour's appendicitis and how Shane had been so homesick. 'I was desperate until I remembered that all we ever hear from next door is country and western music. So I thought Shane might feel more at home if he had something familiar to listen to. I popped next door, borrowed some country and western tapes and, do you know, it did the trick. Come and see.'

Shane was bobbing up and down on his perch and swaying his head to the music. 'Bloody parking ticket,' he remarked when he saw us.

'Isn't he *sweet*?' I said. 'Look at his lovely yellow crest. Do you think he's happy now?'

'Well, I don't know much about birds but I think he must be. He's eating and dancing all the time and he keeps saying bloody parking ticket. How else can one tell?'

'I don't know anything about exotic birds either. Does he really only like country and western?'

'Unfortunately yes. I've tried him on Beethoven, Handel and Bach but it doesn't work. I feel it's better to let him have what he wants while he's here.' Shane watched her with his head on one side and repeated bloody parking ticket a few times. Mrs Herring sighed. 'Shane dear,' she said gently, 'your conversation is a trifle limited. Can't you say pretty Polly for a change?' If Shane did have more phrases in his repertoire he was saving them for a rainy day. As we left the room he was still saying bloody parking ticket.

I've met quite a few 'good neighbour' types through my

121

work. Some of the things they do deserve medals but often they don't even get a thank you. There was a lovely lady, whom I'll call Mrs X because she would be embarrassed to be known, who took in anything that needed a home. As well as bedraggled birds and abandoned cats and dogs she had as a permanent lodger a rather dreadful one-legged ninety-year-old man. You'd have thought that being old *and* legless would have slowed him down a bit but he was so agile that he had been chucked out of several geriatric homes for being unmanageable. He liked to sprint down to the betting shop every morning, collect his winnings from the previous day ('He never seems to back losers,' said Mrs X), then wait for the pubs to open. After a liquid lunch he would back some more horses, then off he would go to the off-licence for tobacco and a bottle of rum to see him through the evening.

All this wouldn't have been so bad but the old boy's real drawback was that he stank to high heaven. He never took a bath and never wanted to change his clothes. Mrs X would have to wait until he was well and truly plastered before she could force him into clean clothes and even though he got through an amazing amount of alcohol he was seldom drunk enough to be cooperative. He was a lucky man to have such a caring landlady but the old horror wasn't a bit grateful. He complained a lot, mainly about his meals which he said gave him toothache. On the one occasion that I met him (I took care to arrange my visits when he was out) he seemed to think I was some sort of para medic. 'What can you do about my toothache?' he demanded.

'Nothing,' I said. 'Why don't you go to a dentist?'

'Anyway, you wear dentures,' Mrs X chipped in. 'Dentures don't give you toothache.'

'That's what you think, my lady,' said the old man, and fished the unlovely objects out of his mouth. Putting them on the table he mumbled something through his gums that I didn't understand.

'Put those nasty teeth back in,' said Mrs X. 'The lady doesn't want to look at them.'

'They're horrible,' I said glancing at them bravely. 'Why

are they orange? I thought false teeth were supposed to be white?'

The old man mumbled some more and Mrs X translated: 'He says he's had them since 1947. They made the gum bits orange in those days.'

'*Forty seven?*' I said. 'But they must be worn out by now. He really should see a dentist.'

Again translating Mrs X said he didn't like dentists and that the teeth would 'see him out'. I had the distinct impression that he was enjoying being the centre of attention so I packed up my things and left before he got round to showing me the stump of his missing leg. It was a pity though that he was so unlikeable because ninety-year-olds with all their marbles can be so interesting to talk to. I once had an eighty-five-year-old friend who had clear memories of his *grandfather*'s tales of his (the grandfather's) boyhood – real living history that was. The grandfather had lived in the village of Kilburn as a boy and knew Marble Arch as Tyburn. I think people should be compelled to keep a logbook the same as you have to with cars.

Chapter Thirteen

SARA'S MARKET STALL in London was doing well but, as Marcus had predicted, standing around outdoors in all weathers was hard going. She had started off selling pure wool chunky knit sweaters, the sort that sell for thirty or forty pounds in the shops (she sold them from twelve pounds) and which were very popular, particularly with Americans. Then, when the weather began to warm up, she branched out into sportswear. She stocked up on tracksuits, T-shirts, shorts, swimwear and jackets with the makers' name emblazoned on the fabric. These were a favourite with teenagers who seem to regard it as some sort of a status symbol to provide free advertising for clothing manufacturers. There was one such lad who coveted a shiny white jacket complete with logo but he couldn't afford it. Sara took him on as a helper (she referred to him as 'my staff' which pleased him) so that he could earn himself the price of the jacket. His name was Mustapha and he was instantly nicknamed Mustavajacket.

Sara worked on a low-profit quick-turnover principle and the sportswear did as well as the sweaters. Soon she had saved enough to take a lease on a small shop. Business was so good that again she took on 'my staff', this time a school leaver called Chris, a most likeable and dependable lad, popular with the customers because being a sports enthusiast himself he knew what gear was needed for what. The name of the shop is Sportswear House and it's in Crouch End, London N.8. Sara gives huge discounts for quantity, so if you are kitting out a school team you couldn't do better than to pay her and Chris a visit. End of commercial.

It was rather strange that Sara should have gone from stallholder to shopkeeper while her parents had done it the other way round. We had gone from retail florist (in London) to

Garden Centre to market stall. There were some other projects in between but basically that was the pattern. Even Marcus is not averse to a bit of selling; whenever he travels from a cold place like the Himalayas to a hot place he sells his equipment and buys new on his return.

We suggested jokingly to Marcus that he should introduce boot sales to the sub-continent (bullock-cart sales? rickshaw sales?) as their popularity over here made it possible for some people to make a small seasonal living from them.

The overheads couldn't be lower – three to four pounds a day plus your petrol – and if you keep your prices down you quickly get a good reputation and a band of regular customers. This is particularly true of home-cooking stalls (known always as cake stalls although as well as cakes they do savoury flans and pies, biscuits, jams, etc.) which are far and away the most popular at any fête, market or boot sale. You can buy the most delicious pies and things to put in the freezer at very little more than it would cost you to make them yourself. I asked one stallholder how she was able to sell so cheaply and still make a profit and she said it was because she cooked a really big batch at a time. 'Take my bacon and egg pies,' she said (the word quiche has not yet reached this outpost of Empire). 'If I make fifty at a time they only cost me about thirty pence so I make a nice profit selling at sixty, don't I?' She went on to tell me she had an Aga and was determined to 'make the old girl work for its living'. Aga owners are so *funny*, on the one hand resenting the very high running costs and on the other almost revering them. I'm sure a learned treatise could be written about the psychology of Agaphiles. My own view is that they're deeply insecure people who need the presence of a big warm mother figure. The real thing – the flesh and blood mothers – have a disconcerting habit nowadays of running off with toy boys or organising treks to Katmandu, but the cast-iron substitute is by its very design, anchored to the home. It can't be coincidence that in order to minister to an Aga's needs you have to kneel . . .

Anyway going back to boot sales, it was nice to meet up with some of our fellow stallholders from the previous

125

year: the Cornish pasty cook, and a young mother who made baby clothes and used her own baby to model the clothes for the customers; several craft persons of indeterminate sex selling pottery and dried flowers, and even our young friend Laurence. He enquired politely after Conrad Onions but his mind was no longer on frogs. 'I'm five and a quarter now,' he said as though people of five and a quarter were so burdened by weighty responsibilities that they had no time to play.

'And have you started school yet?' we asked.

'Yes thank you.'

'Are you enjoying it?'

'Yes thank you.' We thought that was all we were going to hear about it but then in a rush of confidence he said, 'Do you want me to tell you about school?' Trying not to sound too eager we said yes and after a long pause he said reflectively: 'My teacher has got very clean feet.' Another pause. 'Very very clean feet.'

Aching to hear more we craned down to Laurence's level but it was no good, his lips were sealed. We had to pretend to be laughing at something completely different so as not to hurt his feelings.

Converging like soldier ants on every car as it drove in, then frenziedly grabbing every item with resale potential, were the dealers. A new form of pest disguised as bona fide buyers they were *such* a pain in the neck. Most organisers tried to keep them out by putting 'No Dealers' in the boot sale adverts but they still got in and everybody loathed them. As ours was only a plant stall they never bothered us but we felt awfully sorry for sellers who had come for a nice day out and to make a few bob and then found themselves practically under attack from the dealers. 'I'll take this off your hands,' was the phrase that we all hated. The implication that they were doing the seller a favour by buying a 10p trinket was so insulting. This same trinket could well end up *at the same sale* – which was a further insult – on the dealer's own stall marked up to a pound or more.

We saw a dealer come a cropper once, it was lovely and it served him right. A boy of about twelve had set up a stall to sell off his outgrown toys and books, probably because the family was moving house and wanted a big clear out. He had put neat little price stickers on his wares: books at 30p, lots of small cars and trucks at 40p and some toy train accessories also very cheap. The whole lot added up to about ten pounds. The dealer rummaged through the toys then came out with the usual, 'I'll take this lot off your hands for a fiver,' nonsense. The boy said no he would rather sell the things separately whereupon the dealer became quite nasty. Brian and another man who had seen what was going on went over to the boy's stall to give him moral support and it turned out that this other man knew a bit about the value of old toys. He advised the boy to re-price all the Dinky cars and trucks at two pounds and three pounds and to withdraw the Hornby rolling stock altogether. (Apparently old Hornby train accessories are quite rare and best sold through private adverts in enthusiasts' specialist magazines.) The dealer was *most* put out and went away grumbling horribly. The boy was radiant.

It's often funny and sad at the same time to watch teenagers selling their toys. A lot of them do it to raise funds for charity while others see it as a means to an end, a bike maybe or a new cricket bat. They know that they're at a watershed in their lives and that they must discard bears and dolls and Ladybird books but they don't seem to enjoy it very much. Sometimes they go to great lengths *not* to make a sale: 'That jigsaw's got three bits missing,' they'll say, and if the customer still persists in buying it: 'Don't say I didn't warn you.' Parting with stuffed toys can be hard too. 'Bit old for a teddy, aren't you?' 'This ones arm'll keep falling off if you don't keep him dressed.' What a giveaway it is to refer to a teddy as 'him'.

Nearly every Sunday if it wasn't raining there would be a boot sale. This meant that there was never enough time to have the traditional lazy browse through the papers but we kept more or less in touch with things outside Devon by reading our wrapping paper (newspaper) during lulls between customers. Looking at life retrospectively was quite interesting, particularly when we ran out of our own newspapers and began to make use of my mother's hoard. She has a great reverence for the printed word and has never knowingly thrown away a newspaper, so many of our customers found their plants wrapped in old *News Chronicles*. *Very* old. Anyone taking the trouble to smooth out the pages would have learned that the Tirpitz raid had been successful, that Churchill and Roosevelt had had further matey chats, and how you could feed four people on a carrot and an ounce of cheese. Nobody ever commented so either they didn't notice or they didn't want to be reminded that the amount of cheese we all so casually eat *daily* was once a fortnight's ration.

It was in a more current newspaper – only a couple of months old so bang up-to-date by my mother's standard – that I discovered a thought-provoking article. It claimed that 67% of people who attend writers' conferences are suffering from depression. According to the *Observer* someone in America had carried out a survey and I suppose in America the findings may be true. A nation that has given us hamburgers and drum majorettes has got to be suffering from some sort of brain deficiency. So later in the year when Terry asked me if I wanted to go to a writers' conference he was organising in Torquay I told him about the article. He wanted to know if the 67% suffered depression before, after, or because of the conferences. I said the survey hadn't delved all that deeply but that the conclusion was that all writers are neurotic to start with. Terry didn't disagree. He had been organising the Torquay conferences twice a year for years and had a wealth of anecdotes about the people who came. His favourite was about the speaker who fell asleep. 'It was during question time,' he said. 'The questions were so paralysingly dull the speaker just nodded off.'

Another time a writer had brought along a hamster in a cardboard box because she couldn't bear to be parted from it. Instead of leaving it in her bedroom where nobody would have been any the wiser she took it into dinner. One of the other hotel guests had objected and called the manager who had no alternative but to declare the little creature a rodent.

As rodents are not allowed in hotels the hamster was expelled. Its owner was dreadfully upset and threatened to leave too. The manager, caught in the crossfire, was also upset. Peace was only restored when a friend of the hamster owner, a woman who lived in Torquay and was attending the lectures as a day girl, offered to take the animal to her own home.

I wasn't sure if I wanted to go to the conference because broadly speaking I think people who write are better off doing it than talking about doing it. But on the other hand if this year's meeting ran true to form I could observe the proceedings like Malinowski and his Trobriand Islanders and maybe get a saleable article out of it. (The fact that all the other writers would be doing the same thing had not escaped me. Parasites all, we could suck from each other and spit out the husks and if 67% of us got depressed about it that was just hard cheese.)

Having decided to go, I had the bad luck to arrive late – a wheel came off the car in the middle of Torquay and I had to continue on foot – so I took a seat at the back of the conference room. Other latecomers included some people who had come into the hotel foyer to get out of the rain and whose dishevelled appearance for some reason caused the hotel receptionist to assume they were writers and direct them into our meeting. Another late arrival was a girl who was supposed to be attending a geology lecture but by the time she had found out she was in the wrong room she had lost interest in geology and decided to become a writer. 'I hadn't realised it was so easy to write a book,' she said in one of the speaker's breaks. 'It's just words, isn't it?' Someone commented that you have to get the words in the right order but we all knew exactly what the girl meant.

The guest speaker, a well-known novelist, was excellent. She read extracts from some 'work in progress' – a euphemism for 'I'm totally stuck and need a prod to get moving again' and then extracts from some of her published work. Apart from her mania for her word processor which for people like me who can't even use a push-button telephone, was inexplicable, we all enjoyed her lecture very much. She invited members of the audience to read aloud extracts of their own work for criticism. A lot of would-be writers find this sort of exercise helpful but it can be a bit hard on the listeners. If the passage being read is good, it's frustrating not to hear more and if it's bad you sit and fidget and wonder if anyone will have the courage to say how awful it was. (Nobody ever does.)

The speaker had not put a time limit on the individual readers – in later conferences Terry introduced an absolutely essential five-minutes-only rule – so one man went on and on. This would have been OK if the subject had been interesting but his theme was pornographic, all thrust and throb, interspersed with various squelchy words. His description of sexual intercourse could equally well have been that of someone washing the kitchen floor with a long-handled mop. An old lady sitting in the row in front of me knitting a scarf commented loudly: 'I didn't know insects did it like that.' 'Incest,' corrected her neighbour. 'The man's doing it with his sister.'

By God knows what association of ideas I suddenly remembered my car abandoned(?) in Torquay. Before coming to the meeting I'd phoned Brian who was not best pleased to hear that there was a severely handicapped car requiring his attention. Our jack had a nasty habit of slipping and he didn't fancy a squashed foot. He asked me to ask Terry to lend us his jack and we arranged to meet by the car in a couple of hours.

I scribbled a note to Terry who sat at the top table next to the guest speaker and watched its progress as it was passed from hand to hand up to the front. It was interesting to see that published writers automatically read it before sending it on whereas the other ranks didn't. I had written 'Can I borrow your jack, please?' Terry's note came back via the same route: 'I'll do it for you if it's only a wheel.' Born centuries out of his time, Terry has the very endearing notion that the fairer sex shouldn't sully their hands. The porno man, who must have overdosed his central character on ginseng, was still in full spate so Terry and I slipped away quietly.

'Sorry to be a nuisance,' I said, 'but I expect you were quite glad of an excuse to get away from that ghastly old git.'

'Don't talk about my father like that,' said Terry.

'He's *not*?'

'No. Now what's all this about a jack? Have you had a puncture?'

'I don't think so, the wheel came off without any warning.'

Terry insisted on driving me to our lame car. Brian was already there crawling around on all fours searching for wheel nuts. Unfortunately, Terry's jack was the wrong sort for our car so there was nothing for it but to call a garage and get the job done professionally. 'Is it worth the cost of a repair?' Terry asked, peering inside the car with undisguised horror. Hayseeds had germinated in the carpet at the back giving a pleasantly rustic stamp to the interior design. 'Or are you renting it out to a goat?'

Brian sprang to the car's defence, more out of superstition than a belief in its quality; it did after all have a few more weeks' MOT still to run . . .

Back at the hotel the meeting had stopped for a tea break. Brian went to have a wash, and by the time he'd done that, then had a cup of tea and a chat, the warmth and comfort of the hotel proved considerably more attractive than wrestling with a broken car in the rain. So, like the misdirected geologist, he stayed.

In the next session the speaker emphasised the importance of writing about things that you have experienced at first hand. Carefully avoiding the eye of Porno, she said it would sound contrived if you tried to describe pearl fishing on a coral reef when you'd never been further than Stoke-on-Trent. The exception to this rule was science fiction. Since nobody had actually explored distant galaxies the science fiction writer could make up any amount of mumbo-jumbo without getting smug letters from readers pointing out technical errors. After question time there were more readings from the floor. One of the stories was set in ancient Rome. My attention wandered. I mused on the difficulties the Roman soldiers must have had when they washed their leather tunics. They must have taken ages to dry. And those poor Colosseum lions. Didn't they *mind* an unrelieved diet of humans? Did they say, 'Oh hell, not Christians again, we had

131

Christians on Thursday?' The extract ended with polite applause which brought me back with a jolt, followed by criticisms. ('Not too happy about the garrison commander lighting that candle with a box of matches.') Then came the best reading of the day, Sam Sparrow.

Telling a story from a bird's viewpoint couldn't have been easy but Sam's creator had tackled the job with such verve that we, the listeners, were hooked from the start. Sam lived in London, one of a large cockney flock and his story was read in the authentic East End dialect. In the first episode Sam has to escort his small nephew to the country to get some colour into his cheeks. Neither sparrow has ever been to the country before and like the evacuees during the war they have to keep their wits about them so as not to look silly in the eyes of the country birds. The dialogue was fast and witty, Sam's 'Jack the Lad' character irresistible, and the picture of a worried sparrow desperately trying to make sense of the countryside and take care of his scruffy little nephew, original to say the least.

There was prolonged applause and no criticism. Terry brought the session to a close saying it was nice to end on a good note, which I thought was somewhat tactless in view of the Roman centurions. 'Before you all dash off to the bar,' he continued, 'we have to take a vote. I've been through your nominations for the next conference guest speaker and I've short-listed two. Dick Francis or a Mrs Whitby who works as an editor for a London publisher. Can I have a show of hands?' Nearly everybody voted for Mrs Whitby and someone said crossly, 'I thought we were definitely having Dick Francis.'

'Mrs Whitby will be better than Dick Francis,' Terry promised wildly. 'She'll be able to tell you exactly what happens to your manuscripts from the moment you post them.'

'We *know* what happens to them,' said the Dick Francis fan. 'They come back with a rejection slip.' Everyone laughed, scraped back their chairs and made for the bars.

Brian and I sought out Sam Sparrow and his wife, alias Roy and Anne. Like us they were immigrants, Anne from Surrey and Roy from London (coincidentally just one street away from where we had had our flower shop in Holborn) and had settled in Plymouth. We congratulated Roy on Sam Sparrow and learned to our astonishment that he didn't regard Sam as a commercial proposition but more as a party piece to be brought along to functions like this writers' meeting. 'It would make a wonderful radio comedy,' I said. 'Have you done just the one episode or are there more?'

'Twelve,' said Roy. He reminded us of a woman we came across at a car boot sale who was selling a mint condition first edition Kenneth Grahame for £1.50. On that occasion we had done our Karmas no end of good by telling the woman the facts of life as regards first editions. This time though we had no such authority. You can't force a person to hammer on the door of the BBC and demand a hearing for their small sparrow.

An amusing outcome of the writers' conference that none of us had foreseen was the success story of Terry's Aunt Elsie. Terry, like the good nephew he is, had invited Aunt Elsie to come to the lectures to give her a change of scene (she had arthritis and was virtually housebound) and to see some new faces. In she came complete with her knitting and a book in case things got boring and was settled into a comfortable chair. During the refreshment breaks she chatted to a few aspiring writers but other than this she just sat quietly watching and listening to the proceedings. At question time and general discussion she learned that new writers must expect lots of setbacks and disappointments; rejection, particularly in the very competitive field of magazine articles, was the norm and the only way to get published was to keep on trying.

This didn't suit Aunt Elsie's resolute nature at all. Having attended one course of evening classes in upholstery and then immediately re-upholstered all her chairs to a very high standard, she didn't see why exactly the same principle shouldn't apply to writing. Here she was on a writers' course – albeit only a two-day event – therefore she would write something and get it published and never mind that defeatist nonsense about competition. In this frame of mind she went home and wrote two articles for the *Lady* magazine both of which were accepted, paid for and printed straightaway . . .

Terry's remark about our car not being worth the cost of a repair must have mortally offended it because shortly afterwards it got its revenge. It had been an ill-behaved machine for most of the time we'd had it so it came as no surprise when it staged its death scene at an inconvenient time and place, namely in the dark on a public highway. Cars are put together in two halves, the top bit and the bottom bit (there's probably more to it than that but I'm afraid that's the extent of my knowledge) and the bottom is called the sub frame. Everything is held together by enormously strong bolts as you will discover if you ever try to unbolt one, and normally it all stays in one piece. Not always though. Ours separated back to its two component parts. It waited until I was pootling along at about five miles an hour one night then without warning the entire bottom dropped onto the road, the equivalent to a prolapse in biological terms. I *did* feel a fool sitting at road level still strapped in the seat.

Fortunately a couple of policemen came cruising by in a patrol car and they were most helpful. They arranged cones and flickering lanterns all round the dead car so that it looked like an important personage lying in state and then they radioed for a breakdown truck to come and take it away. All the time they were working they were very proper and polite but I could see they were having a job not to laugh. I said, 'It's never done that before,' meaning it had done other things and one of the policemen said he had never seen a whole sub-frame on the road before either. They both speculated several times about 'your hubby' and what was he going to say. 'Tell him it wasn't your fault,' they advised kindly. My hubby needless to say didn't turn a hair. Cars dropped to bits, buttons didn't get sewn on, cats vomited, life was full of minor irritations.

Not long after this, emboldened by the relative security of a new car, Brian announced that he was going to drive to East Anglia. Not non-stop – the car was only new in the sense of being new to us, somebody else had had it for eight years first – but in two stages. 'I'll stop overnight at Reg and Sheila's,' he said, and packed himself a holdall. The trip to East Anglia was sadly to attend an uncle's funeral so item number one to be packed was a suit. Never one to travel light, Brian then proceeded to load the car up with enough equipment to service an expedition to Outer Mongolia. Spanners, torches, maps and a compass, a shovel, food (the journey was motorway all the way), books, a radio – the heap was endless. 'I see you're going to rob a bank on the way,' I said holding up a nylon stocking.

'Put that back, I may need it in case the fan belt breaks.'

I said firmly: 'Nothing can possibly go wrong with a car we've only had five minutes,' and I was right. Nothing went *mechanically* wrong but Reg and Sheila are still dining out on Brian's overnight stay with them.

He got there in time for supper and the three of them had an enjoyable evening. Reg and Brian had known each other since their first day at school together; Brian's mother says Reg hasn't changed in all that time which makes me think he must have been a most unusual five-year-old. The next morning Brian got up early, bathed and shaved, then put on his formal clothes. He made himself a pot of tea and was just about to slip off quietly without waking the others when they heard him and got up to see him on his way.

Brian walked down the path, got into the car and drove off. When he reached the end of their road he realised he had forgotten his jacket. Instead of turning round and going back the way he had come he turned left, left and left again and arrived back at the house a few minutes later. Meanwhile Reg had seen Brian's jacket in the hall and knowing that you can't appear at a funeral half dressed, had grabbed it, jumped in his car and set off in pursuit. When he reached the end of the road he turned right and seeing no sign of Brian's car carried on driving, right up to and on to the motorway. At this point he remembered he was wearing only his pyjamas . . .

On the principle of 'in for a penny' he continued to give chase. Twenty miles up the motorway he guessed that Brian must have gone back. He slowed down, hoping it wouldn't be too far to the next exit point but he was unlucky and it was a good three quarters of an hour before he arrived back home. And as by now the world was up and about its business he had to cover the distance from car to front door – still in his pyjamas – in full public gaze. He found Sheila and Brian sitting in the kitchen holding their aching sides. Neither of them can now recall Reg's actual words when he came in. Probably just as well.

Chapter Fourteen

THE VOGUE OF EXCHANGE visits between British and foreign children must be one of the surest ways of getting quite the worst of both worlds. Swapping one's teenage louts for a new wheelbarrow or a decent dinner service would be one thing but swapping them for someone else's equally ghastly offspring has got to be the last word in masochism. From time to time we helped out on Raymond and Valerie's Open Days (they raised money for charity six Sundays a year by opening their gardens to the public) and when the visitors filed in you could always spot a family with an exchange student from the host mother's expression. Sometimes you could even guess how the visit was going and how many days it still had to run. At the start mothers would be bright and breezy and at the finish would often draw upon reserves of strength and become bright and breezy again, but in between they were just plain fed up with the whole thing. The young guests, who seemed to be mainly French, were almost invariably of the sullen variety. This is not to say that our own homegrown teenagers aren't sullen too but the French seem to have perfected the smouldering sulk almost to an art form. There was one family I remember in particular because their French guest, a boy of about sixteen, broke union rules and was seen to smile.

Helen, a friend of Valerie's, and I were serving cream teas on one of the lawns at Hill House one Sunday and as usual getting in a fine old muddle with the prices – like me Helen is fine in the shallows of arithmetic but that's as far as it goes – when in came a family of four, mother, father, son and French boy. The father was making hearty noises of approval about the nursery and gardens, the son was immersed in a book, the French boy was in one of the aforementioned sulks and the mother was wittering away about what a nice time they were all having. Helen took their order. 'My husband and I would like cream teas, please . . .' Helen wrote down 2 CT '. . . and Richard would like – Richard do come out of that book for a moment and tell us what you'd like.' Richard gave a few primitive grunts which his mother translated: 'He says cream tea and some of that delicious chocolate cake, please. Now, Sacha dear, would you like to choose?' Sacha dear had no intention of displaying any pretty party manners. In his best Smoulder he scowled at the scones and cream which a couple on the next table were tucking into and muttered, *'Vachement moche.'*

'Oh *we* call it Devon cream tea,' said his hostess blithely. 'I don't suppose you have anything like it in Rouen, do you?' Helen, who knew precisely what *vachement moche* meant, saw the flicker of a smile on Sacha's face before he remembered to smoulder again. And the smoulder became a groan when he at last came out with what he wanted and Helen said we didn't do coke, only tea or coffee. 'Don't grumble, Sacha,' said the mother. 'With your acne you shouldn't really go in for so much sugar.' And then she added obscurely: 'Besides it's in aid of charity. That's ch-ar-it-y. What's charity in French, Richard?' Richard ignored her and carried on reading. The father said apropos of absolutely nothing: 'That's the ticket, old man, always safest to go native,' and Helen, completely bemused by the pointlessness of the conversation, gave them four cream teas with extra cake for Richard and left them to 'enjoy' their day out.

That particular Open Day was in aid of the Gardeners' Benevolent Fund, a charity which looks after ageing gardeners when they're too crocked up to work. Brian, who frequently feels he would qualify as a candidate for assistance, was on the gate taking the entry money. One man stopped when he saw the charity poster and said, 'What's all this? I don't normally pay to come here.'

'It's fifty pence to look round the gardens today,' Brian said and in case the man couldn't read added. 'They're collecting for the Gardeners' Benevolent Fund.'

'Bugger that for a game of soldiers,' said the man and

138

left. But nobody else minded the small admission charge and the grounds thronged with people. The nursery had come out top in a *Gardening Which* report on specialist pinks nurseries while the house and grounds had been the subject of a chapter in a recently published book on vicarage gardens. All in all, Hill House was enjoying a modest fame in the horticultural world so when a small boy approached Brian and said, 'Excuse me sir, are you someone important?' Brian assumed that he wanted to ask a question about gardening. 'Fire away,' he said, 'and if I can't help you I'm sure Mr Hubbard can.'

'Well sir, I wondered if you happen to have a book on rare carp.'

'*Rare carp?*' Brian was flummoxed. 'I'm awfully sorry but I don't think they keep any books on fish.' The boy looked disappointed. Brian said curiously, 'What do you want to know about rare carp?'

'Well you see, sir, there are some specimens in Mr Hubbard's lake which I can't identify. I thought I might look them up while I'm waiting.'

Making a mental note to tell Raymond and Valerie that their goldfish pond had been promoted to lake Brian said, 'Waiting for what?'

'For my parents, sir. They're always looking round stately homes but I'm afraid I get so bored I just leave them to it.'

'Oh,' said Brian wondering what Ray and Val would say when they heard that the house as well as the pond had been upgraded. He also wondered how he could stop the child calling him sir. 'Look, um, what's your name?'

'Pagett, sir.'

'What do your friends call you?'

'Pagett, sir.'

Brian gave up and directed young Pagett over to Raymond who was only too pleased of an excuse to get away from a group of visitors who had buttonholed him and were asking the same old questions. (Running a stately home can be exhausting at times.) Together they made for the goldfish pond and lay on their stomachs looking over the edge.

Helen and I continued to fall over each other in the kitchen but none of the customers complained about being kept waiting or having the wrong bill. At one point the supply of scones ran out. We were all for letting them eat cake but Valerie, popping into the house to get a tray of tea for all the helpers, said we would find another batch in the top right-hand corner of one of the freezers. I always get a terrible sense of inadequacy when people talk about what's in their freezer with such confidence. I've met women who can welcome four unexpected guests with 'No problem, my loves, I'll just defrost something.' Awesome really. *Their* pre-cooked dishes never look like something which has disagreed with someone else first. Thank heaven for fish and chip shops, I say.

The day went well and quite a lot of money was raised. The following Sunday saw us all assembled again only this time it was pouring with rain. You wouldn't imagine people would want to tour vicarage gardens in the rain but in fact there was the same number of visitors as the previous Sunday. I think maybe holidaymakers like an element of risk when they're away from home – muggings in America, alligators in Africa, pneumonia in England – it all adds to the fun. 'I love it here,' said one woman, 'it's so homely.' As she was standing ankle-deep in a puddle at the time, surrounded by piles of flowerpots which Raymond hadn't yet got round to stacking (in his own domain he isn't as organised as Valerie), it made us wonder what her home was like. By 'homely' she may have meant welcoming. Ray and Val have a knack of making every single customer feel that he or she is the most important person there. While this undoubtedly boosts sales and gives everyone a nice warm glow the price in units of boredom can be high. A man once pinned Ray down for twenty minutes going on about what to plant in a *window box*! And when the vicarage gardens book came out there was a whole new species of bore, people who seemed to think that because Raymond and Valerie had been the subject of a book they were experts in the literary field. Positively the only thing to say to people who inflict the plot of their unwritten novel on you is sod off, but Ray is too kind for this, on top of which

Valerie says that if they did they wouldn't have any customers left. But she must have been exaggerating.

Not having reputations as good listeners Helen and I enjoyed the customers at one remove as it were. For this rainy day Valerie had set up tables in the house and we served the teas in two of the reception rooms. Valerie's new puppy, a spaniel collie cross called Tate, thought indoor cream teas was a wonderful idea and offered her services as a waitress. She wasn't much good at clearing tables but made up for it by hoovering the floor. Everyone made a great fuss of her and she came in for some forbidden treats which Valerie allowed as it was only once in a blue moon. One tea customer who didn't want Tate hanging round their table was a young mother with a little girl whom she described as hydro-active. 'For lor's sake don't show 'er a puppy,' she pleaded in broad Cornish. 'It'll only yearn 'er for one of 'er own.' Sure enough the little girl set up the immediate '*Please*, Mum' which all of us must have gone through at some stage. She was well and truly yearned all right and we had to shut Tate in the kitchen until the family had finished.

Some other customers who made us laugh were two women talking about a third. The first said: 'Pity Lucy couldn't come today. You knew she sprained her ankle?'

'Oh I am sorry,' said the second. 'Wet leaves?'

'No,' said the first, 'she fell over a piece of Camembert.' And her companion, instead of asking what the cheese was doing on the floor in the first place, said simply: 'They'll *have* to get a bigger house.'

Later in the week Helen asked us to her house to have a look at one of her chickens which wasn't well. She kept four ex-battery hens in her garden. Sometimes they laid, sometimes they didn't but Helen and her husband Piers didn't really mind either way as long as the birds were happy. Brian and I don't know much about poultry but we examined the sick one and could find nothing physically wrong. 'She's so miserable,' said Helen. 'She's been like this for some days now, she seems to have lost interest in living.'

'We had a cockerel that died of an inferiority complex once,' said Brian. 'He wasn't as handsome as our other cockerel and he just sort of faded away.'

'Oh that's very helpful Brian, thank you,' said Piers. 'Are you suggesting this is a job for the Samaritans?'

'No, the vet.'

'She's been to the vet. He couldn't find anything wrong either.'

Not long afterwards the little hen died. Helen took the body to the Ministry laboratories for a post mortem. The duty vet shared her concern: an inexplicable death is best investigated in case it's due to something contagious. Pen poised over his form the vet asked Helen how many birds she kept. 'Four,' said Helen.

'Would that be four hundred or four thousand?'

'Just four. We haven't the room for any more in our garden.'

The vet laid down his pen. 'Four,' he repeated, and thought for a moment. 'We normally investigate problems from, er, rather larger units.'

'Oh.'

'But never mind. I'll put down that a quarter of your flock is affected.'

Which all goes to show how misleading statistics can be. The post mortem report recorded death from natural causes. A chicken's brain is approximately the size of a postage stamp but even with this limitation I'm sure they are capable of making some decisions. Helen's had plainly got up one morning in a foul mood, looked out at the endless rain and decided that really life wasn't worth the effort. Turkeys do this sort of thing sometimes only they don't do it quietly. If they take offence at something, they are capable of leaping dramatically into the air and dropping dead with no warning at all. Perhaps the Samaritans *should* branch out into poultry.

With all the practice I'd been having at adding up the tea customers' bills the elementary arithmetic required at a village whist drive should have been a doddle. Brian and I like the occasional game of cards so when we saw a notice advertising a fund-raising whist drive at a local school we went along.

Country whist drives are the most enormous fun and a cheap night out at 60p a head with refreshments at half time. This one was no exception and we had the added bonus, because it was staged in one of the classrooms, of literary diversions pinned up on the wall. The set subject of that week's composition was An Accident. (We guessed this as all fifteen of the stories on the wall were headed An Accident.)

'Once upon a time there was a woodcutters son from humble oranges . . .' we read. Oh dear. It was easy to guess what sort of accident *this* was going to be. But no. The woodcutter's oranges were not that humble. He possessed a chainsaw, no less, and despite the fact that he was 'very Karefull' with it his idiotic son managed to get too near the business end, losing 'both his thums' in the process.

Leaving the child in the capable hands of the disstrek nurse we moved on to the other stories. Some of the spelling was incredible – pure Chaucer. We saw hospital written as orzbl (if you say it out loud, it's actually quite straightforward phonetic spelling – West Country style) but this same child had got Massey Ferguson correct to the letter. As to content, well these cautionary tales were quite an eye-opener. Apart from the chainsaw mishap there were accidents involving tractors, conveyor belts and milk tankers on the transport side; bulls, dogs, ferrets and rats in the animal range, plus miscellaneous shotguns and slurry tank disasters. Did the mothers of these children, I wondered, send them on holiday to inner-city no go areas where the occasional mugger or rapist would seem small beer compared to the hazards of the farmyard?

The bell rang for us to take our seats. Clutching my pink card with LADY printed across the top – what women's libbers would make of whist drives I dread to think – I sat down opposite a Gentleman (his card was white entitled GENT) and we silently summed each other up. Progressive whist is a curious game, one minute you and your partner are in a situation of utmost intimacy then, once the hand is played, you separate and start all over again with a different partner. As one woman, sorry – Lady, put it, it's

143

like being a Plymouth prostitute when a troopship comes in.

The play was breathtakingly fast. Forget about Las Vegas or Monte Carlo if you want to see cards played at speed – just try Devon. Flick flick flick *trump*, flick flick flick *lose*; both pairs of players alternating between despair and elation as the tricks pile up. Then the quick reckoning of the score – quick for everybody except one whose brain goes outside to wait for her in the car as soon as simple addition is required. The two sets of opponents sign each others' scorecards to prevent cheating; if any of my opponents *did* want to cheat they would have no difficulty with me checking their sums . . . 'Pardon me mentioning it, m'dear, but do ee always count backwards?' said my partner, kindly drawing my attention to a small error on my card. Confronted with 45 + 8 I had made a wild guess and put 33.

At half time there was tea and cake. Someone went to the loo and came back to report that the cistern had fallen off the wall when she pulled the chain, causing a medium-sized flood on the floor. The school caretaker, who was doubling as tea dispenser, went out to fix it leaving the accident-prone lady in charge of the tea urn. 'Tempting providence, aren't you?' somebody commented. Everyone fell about laughing. You really don't need alcohol to get a party spirit going, a steamy urn and a plumbing setback does the trick nicely. 'Ooh, I do loves a night out,' giggled a farmer's wife whose glowing red cheeks suggested a lifetime of 'out'. Her companions nodded, refilled their cups and said it was better than the telly if you wanted a proper laugh.

Some of us took our tea and went back to finish reading the children's compositions. I was intrigued by one which *ended* with the sentence: 'The vet cleared his throat.' Now, in my ignorance, I'd always thought that if a person in a story clears his throat the reader can confidently expect some sort of pronouncement to follow. Not so. I had to read the story from the beginning before the penny dropped. Once upon a time (these Hans Andersen openings were very popular) a farmer

144

had an Aberdeen Angus bullock which swollerd a piece of wire. The young author had then made the mistake of going into a detailed technical description of the vet's car instead of staying with the medical emergency. However all ended well. '. . . the engine stopped and he got out with his bag. The vet cleared his throat. The End.'

Chapter Fifteen

ALTHOUGH I DON'T expect a fanfare of trumpets when I call at the houses of my dog customers I was a bit taken aback one morning when the lady of the house opened the door, looked at me and gasped with horror. 'Are you the dog clipper?' she said and I said yes although strictly speaking the clipper is the machine not the person.

'Have I come on the wrong day or something?' I asked. 'You seem surprised to see me.'

She said accusingly: 'You're dressed in *red*.'

'Oh God, I thought, why do I always seem to get the nutters. I was wearing a red-towelling track suit (from Sara's shop), nice and bright and very comfortable for working in. 'I like red,' I said. 'It's cheerful.'

'That's as may be, but I'm afraid it's quite unsuitable. George has a weak heart,you see, and that shade of red would over-excite him. Haven't you brought an overall?'

'Yes I have, but hang on a minute. You didn't tell me he had a bad heart when you made the appointment. Clipping him might be too stressful.'

'*Jacko* hasn't got a weak heart. It's George – my husband.'

Speaking very slowly so as not to collapse in hysterics on the doorstep I promised not to over-excite her husband. (Some hopes. A stone overweight and reeking of cocker spaniel I couldn't see myself inflaming the passions of anyone except maybe a Crufts fanatic.) Doubtfully she let me in and waited in the hall while I peeled off my red top and replaced it with my overall, a safely green garment. Then and only then was I allowed into the living quarters. It was a tiny house with a galley-type kitchen. I nearly always clip dogs in kitchens – easier to clear up the fur afterwards – but this one was much too small and I was shown into a sitting room instead. Husband George sat at a table reading a newspaper while Jacko, a dear little 57-varieties dog, dozed at his feet. Introductions were made and again I had an awful job not to giggle as the wife was still patently concerned about the possible effect my redness would have on George. He was much older than his missus and if he did have a weak heart there was no sign of it in his firm handshake. Mrs George kept repeating, 'You *will* be careful, won't you?' as I unpacked my tools and stood little Jacko up on the table for his trim. Her tension was catching. Jacko whined, I dropped a comb and George thumped the table with his fist. 'Will you stop your *worrying*, woman,' he roared. Mrs George, who probably meant well turned to me and said: 'You see? I knew this would happen if I let you in.'

Despite his age and infirmity George was master in his own home and defused the situation by ordering her to the kitchen to make some coffee. 'Treats me like an invalid,' he grumbled when she had gone. I couldn't very well take sides as I was only there for the dog but I did feel a bit aggrieved having to take the blame for his outburst. Thinking it might neutralise things I asked him what he had done for a living before he retired. George said: 'Oh, a nice girl like you wouldn't want to hear about my work,' a remark guaranteed to make me really curious. Whatever would a nice girl not want to know about? Pimp? Drug pusher? After a while Mrs George came back with coffee on a tray. 'I was just asking your husband about his work,' I said. She gave such a shriek of disapproval I guessed I'd said something wrong. 'I *told* you to be careful,' she scolded. 'He's not to get fussed with his heart.'

After George had called her a silly cow and she had flounced out in a huff George and I spent the next half hour discussing things connected with his work and very interesting it was too. He had been an embalmer. I swiftly demoted myself from nice girl to avid audience and was even able to cap some of his anecdotes with some from my own days in the floristry trade. Our shop had been next door to an undertaker's which was not only mutually convenient for business but also gave us – via a highly entertaining mole in their camp – a glimpse of the mistakes that occur from time to time in the funeral trade.

'What about this latest lark then?' countered George. 'This aerial burial.'

'What's that?'

'Well, it's like being buried at sea only they do it out of aeroplanes.'

'They wouldn't be allowed, would they? Think of the mess.'

'*Ashes* you daft ha'porth. They scatter the ashes from a plane.'

This was the brainchild of an enterprising pilot somewhere in Scotland who had hit upon the idea as a means of earning a living. The family of the deceased choose a spot that he or she had been particularly fond of and hire young Biggles to fly them up to scatter the ashes over the area. It was all going to be very tasteful with a Presbyterian minister or whatever on board to say the right things. Unfortunately Biggles forgot to make any practice runs beforehand and his first job was not what you'd call a howling success. All was going well until the time came to disperse the ashes over the chosen place. Biggles pulled a lever which was supposed to release the ashes *underneath* the plane but something went wrong and, to his horror, the powdered up dear departed backfired *into* the plane and covered the relatives' faces like talc.

Mrs George disapproved of all the merriment coming from the sitting room and when she paid me she said she would not be requiring my services again. I was sorry. Customers like old George enliven the working day no end.

At the nursery the others had their share of light relief too. There was a young mother who instructed her newborn baby in the pram to 'stay there' and another woman who had a rather unusual burglary story. She and her husband had been woken up at 3 a.m. by the sound of burglars downstairs. Her husband naturally wanted to phone the police immediately but she made him wait so that she would be sure to have her make-up on before they arrived. (Luckily the burglars were only beginners so they got caught despite the delay.) One of Brian's favourite stories was of seeing two little girls, all of five years old, greeting

148

each other after what appeared to be a long separation. One said to the other 'well *you're* a face from the past I must say'. Her friend looked puzzled so she went on 'Don't you remember me? We used to go to the same playgroup.' And my own favourite was also about a child, a boy this time, aged about six or seven. Having been dragged unwillingly to a wedding in the church next to Hill House he had to be removed during the ceremony because of his endless fidgeting.

The young man who brought him out decided to kill time by looking round the nursery. He started chatting to Brian and in the course of the conversation happened to mention that the bride was being given away by her brother. Brian looked down and there was the little boy staring at them open-mouthed. 'Given away?' he echoed, 'By her *brother*?' He was so exhilarated by this apparently perfect solution to sibling trouble that neither of the grown-ups had the heart to spoil it for him.

It was now getting towards the end of the summer and on the last of the charity open days Helen and I had a bumper crop of awkward customers. One woman insisted on having a table to herself as she was receiving messages and didn't want to be disturbed. When we said what messages she told us that one of her fillings in a back tooth picked up signals from outer space. 'They don't speak any earth language,' she said although neither of us had suggested that they did. 'And I find it very hard to concentrate if I'm surrounded by people.'

'But if you can't understand their language what are you concentrating *on*?' I asked. It was a bit annoying to have a table which seated four occupied by just one.

She gave me a withering look. 'I'm concentrating on the bleeps. It must be some sort of code and one of these days I'm going to be able to decode it.' When we took her her tea she complained that the biscuits weren't the right sort, too hard for her precious filling. I said: 'Dip them in your tea then,' and she said she wouldn't dream of doing anything so common. Helen, who is extremely kind and patient, swapped the biscuits for fairy cakes while I expressed myself in an earth language which couldn't have been more common.

Somehow we squeezed all the other customers in (by saying that the extraterrestrial woman's table was reserved) and then had more complaints. This time it was bird droppings – not on the tea tables which would have been justified, but on a family car. Before coming in the husband had parked under some trees for the shade and then blown his top because his parking spot happened to be directly underneath a flock of crows. Although I've seen far too many live lambs with their eyes pecked out by crows to have any affection for the horrible creatures I really didn't think that their loose bowels were anything to get worked up about. 'It's a churchyard,' I said to the irate car owner (car worshipper?) 'A lot of churchyards are rookeries.'

'It's disgusting,' he fumed. 'Quite disgusting. Do you realise that their droppings are *acid*? My paintwork will corrode.'

'I'm here to serve teas,' I said snappily. 'Not to discuss bird shit.'

Helen, meanwhile, had been caught by some horsey girls who wanted her opinion on whether or not a young carthorse would benefit by being chained to its mother during its early training. Helen said yes it would definitely be best. She had never trained anything bigger than her own dog but guessed that a carthorse's mother would be wiser than all the horsey girls put together. Then Raymond came in to say did we know we had a mad Martian taking up a whole table while there were people waiting to sit down. Helen said: 'She's not a real Martian, she's someone with a filling that gives off coded signals.'

'Receives coded signals,' I corrected. Raymond didn't bat an eyelid but reminded us that today was for charity funds so the Martian would have to budge up and make room for earthlings with money to spend. Thinking that Americans would be less likely to mind someone phoning outer space we picked out three ladies from a coachload and sure enough they didn't mind at all. Again and again they said what a perfectly lovely time they were having; a genu-ine English vicarage garden with a genu-ine eccentric to talk to. Their coach party had had a guided tour of

150

Totnes the previous day and these three had been bowled over by the town. In their guidebook Brutus was quoted as saying, as he sailed up the River Dart: 'Here I be and here I rest. And the name of this place shall be called Totnes.' Leaving aside the unlikelihood of an invading Roman soldier spouting verse, I felt sure the utterance must have lost something in translation. Brutus had been cooped up in a crowded ship for weeks and would have been far more likely to say what time do the pubs open, or let's get on with some raping and pillaging. But the Americans thought it kinda cute and as it was their guidebook and their holiday I shut up.

Another aspect of Totnes that they loved was the narrowness of the streets. At the top of the town – appropriately called The Narrows – they had photographed the pavements because they said their friends back home simply wouldn't believe in such incy sidewalks (9½ inches) without proof. They had been up to the castle and round the ramparts, into the Guildhall and over the Roman bridge, and tomorrow they were going by boat to Agatha Christie's riverside garden and then on to see Dartmouth Naval College from the estuary. Whew. Brian and I have done all these things but over two years not two days. No stamina, that's our trouble.

While our energetic visitors were cataloguing their travels the mad Martian was regarding them with mixed feelings. It looked to us as though she wanted to be stand-offish (she had heard herself referred to as a genu-ine eccentric) but at the same time she wanted an audience. When Helen took more hot water out for their teapots she reported that all four of them seemed to be getting on like a house on fire. 'They're on to flying saucers,' she said comfortably. 'A lot better than bird shit as a subject, don't you agree?'

At the end of the six weeks it was good to learn that despite foul weather and awkward customers it had all been worthwhile. Two charities, the Gardeners' Benevolent Fund and the MacMillan Nurses each received a substantial cheque and the nursery itself became more widely known. Later in the year it was even the subject of a television gardening programme.

Nobody watching the programme would have guessed what a panic it was getting the place straight before the filming began. Valerie pressed every available friend into service and at one point in the day there were literally more helpers than customers – grass cutters, hedge cutters, glasshouse washers, gravel rakers, weeders and hoers and pruners. The irony was that when the film was made, and Raymond interviewed in close up, it was his sweater (hand-knitted by Valerie's mother) that stole the show. Valerie said plaintively 'Didn't anyone notice the *garden*?' and we all said blow the garden, where did he get that lovely sweater?

Brian is always puzzled by people who don't understand the principles of growing. Planting, transplanting, feeding and watering are as automatic to him as breathing. You just *know* when to sow and when to thin, etc. So when Marcus wrote to say he was going to the Philippines to grow crops and could Brian tell him how to do it, Brian didn't quite know where to start.

Marcus had a friend who had bought an island. Having bought an island he and Marcus went into town by boat and bought some sacks of grain. And that was it. Neither lad appeared to have the foggiest notion of the bit in between the purchase of the seed and the gathering of the harvest. Brian re-read the letter and groaned. 'He doesn't even say what *sort* of grain let alone anything about the soil or the climate. All he says is "we shall have crops".'

'I think it's very nicely put,' I said defensively.

'I'm criticising his gardening not his writing. Look, there's no mention of buying a spade or a hoe on their shopping spree. Does he think these mysterious grains are going to leap out of the sacks and plant themselves?' Still grumbling he looked out some gardening books and parcelled them up to send express post together with a letter requesting more details about the project.

In due course back came Marcus's reply. The books had arrived safely and were proving useful. Marcus had sprained his ankle but it didn't matter because he and his friend had found a group of old women happy to prepare the soil for them *at £1.50 a day*. Anticipating our outraged reply Marcus had added: 'We're not exploiting them, £1.50 is more than the going rate.'

While these decrepit old souls were toiling away in the sun Marcus had taken his ankle to convalesce in a cool place in the hills. There was a photo: This is me diving through rainbows. He had found a pool, deep enough for swimming and fed by a huge waterfall which caught the sun's rays in such a way as to produce dazzling prisms of light. 'You haven't lived until you know how it feels to dive through rainbows.'

Follow that, as they say. We did have a magic story to tell but it wasn't in the same league as his. We'd been for a walk with the dogs and had come down off the moor into some woodland when we heard the sound of children singing. We stopped and listened as the voices grew louder then along the path came a procession of little children all in fancy dress and leading a pony. One of them was done up as a dough-nut which was just as well or we really would have thought we were dreaming. Doughnuts don't have quite the same aura of magic as elves and pixies. Their pony was in fancy dress too with garlands of flowers round its head and all four hooves painted a different colour. As ever on these occasions we had forgotten the camera but neither of us will ever forget the enchantment. We asked the children if they were going to have a picnic in the woods. They said they were and one added: 'But if it rains we're going to Newton Abbot.' Which is what I meant by our magic not being in the same league as Marcus's.

One morning not too long after this a man from the Council knocked at our door and asked if he could take some readings. When we said *what* readings he unpacked a case containing a tripod and a tape recorder. 'Got to measure your decibels,' he explained, and when we still looked mystified: 'The council's going to build a road. You don't mean to say you haven't heard?'

Brian said we had heard a rumour of a proposed road when we'd move in but hadn't paid much attention and what had decibels got to do with the public highways department?

'Noise,' said the man enigmatically.

I believe all civil servants are required to sign the official secrets act as a condition of their employment, nonetheless we persevered. 'There isn't any noise here,' said Brian. 'We live up a quiet lane.' (He actually said 'up a quite lane' because that's how we'd seen it written by an estate agent and the phrase had become a habit.)

'It *is* quiet, isn't it?' said the man. 'You'll get Benefits I dare say. As he set up his listening equipment he put us in the picture. Everyone living in the vicinity of a potentially noisy new enterprise, whether it's an airfield, a factory or a road, has the right to apply for a rate reduction. In this case all the houses in the neighbourhood were to be measured for noise before and after the road was built. The difference in decibel level would be the measure of the amount of inconvenience suffered.

He switched on the decibel recorder and left, saying he would be back in a few hours. In that time we were amused to see that the needle hardly flickered from the 0 position – even a blackbird singing its heart out in a nearby apple tree couldn't budge it. Obviously we would be in line for Benefits.

But benefits with a small 'b' came from quite another source. Hot on the heels of the man from the council (a year later to be precise but that's fast in Devon) came builders falling over each other with offers for our suddenly highly desirable property. It seems that where there are roads there are also people who want to build houses for people who *like* living near roads. As we had no intention of remaining in the flight path of noisy traffic – with or without a rate reduction – we listened to their proposals and graciously decided to accept an offer from the highest bidder. As we said to Marcus in our next letter you don't necessarily

154

have to go to exotic places to find what's at the end of a rainbow.

P.S. But we would appreciate it Marcus if you'd come home and help us move the four million worms.